In this book Brian Crow and Chris Banfield provide an introduction to post-colonial theatre by concentrating on the work of major drama- tists from the Third World and subordinated cultures in the First World. Crow and Banfield consider the plays of such writers as Wole Soyinka and Athol Fugard and his collaborators from Africa; Derek Walcott from the West Indies; August Wilson and Jack Davis, who write from and about the experience of black communities in the USA and Australia respectively; and Badal Sircar and Girish Karnad from India. Although these dramatists reflect diverse cultures and histories, they share the common condition of cultural subjection or oppression, which has shaped their theatres. Each chapter contains an informative list of primary source material and further reading about the dramatist.

An introduction to post-colonial theatre

CAMBRIDGE STUDIES IN MODERN THEATRE

Series editor
Professor David Bradby, *Royal Holloway, University of London*
Advisory board
Martin Banham, *University of Leeds*
Jacky Bratton, *Royal Holloway, University of London*
Tracy Davis, *Northwestern University*
Richard Eyre, *Director, Royal National Theatre*
Michael Robinson, *University of East Anglia*
Sheila Stowell, *University of Birmingham*

Volumes for Cambridge Studies in Modern Theatre explore the political, social and cultural functions of theatre while also paying careful attention to detailed performance analysis. The focus of the series is on political approaches to the modern theatre with attention also being paid to theatres of earlier periods and their influence on contemporary drama. As a cultural art form, theatre is not produced in a vacuum, rather, it is influenced, whether directly or in more subtle ways, by the political and social environment. In turn, theatre leaves its mark on society, and contributes to shaping that society's level of political awareness. Topics in the series are chosen to investigate this relationship and include both playwrights (their aims and intentions set against the effects of their work) and process (with emphasis on rehearsal and production methods, the political structure within theatre companies, and their choice of audiences or performance venues). Further topics will include devised theatre, agitprop, community theatre, para-theatre and performance art. In all cases the series will be alive to the special cultural and political factors operating in the theatres they examine.

Books published
Brian Crow with Chris Banfield, *An introduction to post-colonial theatre.*

An introduction to
post-colonial theatre

Brian Crow with Chris Banfield

CAMBRIDGE
UNIVERSITY PRESS

Published by the Press Syndicate of the University of Cambridge
The Pitt Building, Trumpington Street, Cambridge CB2 1RP
40 West 20th Street, New York, NY 10011-4211, USA.
10 Stamford Road, Oakleigh, Melbourne 3166, Australia

First published 1996

Printed in Great Britain at Bell & Bain Ltd, Glasgow

A catalogue record for this book is available from the British Library

Library of Congress cataloguing in publication data

Crow, Brian.
An introduction to post-colonial theatre / Brian Crow with Chris Banfield.
    p.   cm. – (Cambridge studies in modern theatre)
Includes bibliographical references.
ISBN 0 521 49529 6 (hardback)
1. Drama – History and criticism.
2. Literature and society – Developing countries.
3. Imperialism.   4. Oppression (Psychology).
I. Banfield, Chris.   II. Title.   III. Series.
PN1643.c76   1996
809.2′9358–dc20   95-13967 CIP

ISBN 0 521 49529 6 hardback
ISBN 0 521 56722 x paperback

For Margaret and Bill Crow

and for Vayu Naidu

Contents

Preface

A characteristic feature of the development of Western art forms during the twentieth century has been the frequent and highly fruitful exploitation by artistic practitioners of all kinds of materials drawn from non-Western cultures. This is as true of the theatre as it is of music, painting and sculpture. For example, a profound influence on Artaud's formulation of the Theatre of Cruelty was, famously, his discovery of Balinese dance-drama at the Paris Colonial Exhibition of 1931. Brecht seems to have discovered what epic acting could be only after he watched the Chinese actors of Mei Lan-fang's company in Moscow in 1935. More recently, two of the most influential figures in contemporary theatre, Jerzy Grotowski and Peter Brook, have drawn much of their inspiration from their encounters with the theatre of non-Western cultures – Grotowski mainly from Indian classical dance-drama, Brook from a variety of Oriental and African sources.

Creatively stimulating though these non-Western influences on European and American theatre have evidently been, one can ask legitimate questions about the extent to which Western practitioners have considered, understood or even much cared about the nature and significance of their borrowings in relation to their original cultural contexts. In this respect, as Rustom Bharucha and others have shown, the stylistic exploitation of, say, Indian forms of theatre has been largely opportunistic and culturally unequal, determined by the perceived needs of Western practitioners and audiences rather than by a genuine effort to confront Indian realities as they are refracted through its rich theatrical culture. This is not to say that the last few years have not witnessed an encouraging growth of appreciation, in an increasingly multicultural context, of non-Western performance complementing the rise of 'world music' and of non-European fine arts. But it *is* to suggest that audiences and readers in the West have still much to discover about both the traditional and contemporary drama and theatre of what we have come to know as the Third World.

This book seeks to make a contribution to that process by introducing the work of some of the leading dramatists of that world. An initial word of explanation is required here, however; for though playwrights such as Wole Soyinka, Derek Walcott, Badal Sircar and Girish Karnad all come from and write about what we normally think of as Third World societies (Nigeria, the West Indies and India, respectively), this is not true of some of the other practitioners we consider: Athol Fugard, John Kani and Winston Ntshona from South Africa, Jack Davis from Australia or August Wilson from the USA. Each of these countries, of course, has a colonial history, which profoundly affected its subsequent social, political and cultural development. Even the USA, which is more usually thought of as itself the major neocolonial power of the twentieth century, has a literature and drama that emerged from the distinctive experiences and tensions of colonization. As the authors of a recent influential book on post-colonial literary theory observe, America's 'relationship with the metropolitan centre as it evolved over the last two centuries has been paradigmatic for post-colonial literatures everywhere'.[1] Nevertheless these are countries whose white populations and cultures, at least, are very much of the 'First' World, as are their 'mainstream' theatre and other arts. How, then, can dramatists from them be regarded as other than First World writers, or meaningfully grouped with dramatists from, for example, Nigeria or India?

The crucial point here is that as former colonies of white settlement these countries have indigenous or imported slave populations whose historically oppressed and relatively impoverished lives may appropriately be described as the Third World within the First. The condition common to all the dramatists considered here is in fact that of cultural subjection or subordination. (Fugard is

---

[1] Bill Ashcroft, G. Griffiths and H. Tiffin, *The Empire Writes Back: Theory and Practice in Post-Colonial Literatures*, London: Routledge, 1989, p. 2.

exceptional in that, though he belongs by race to the dominators, in his artistic practice and his dissenting politics he has consistently taken the side of the oppressed.) Central to their experience of life – and thus to their art – is the knowledge that their people and culture have not been permitted a 'natural' historical development, but have been disrupted and dominated by others.

This is, of course, only one of several possible ways of offering an introduction to post-colonial drama and theatre. But inasmuch as the condition of cultural domination and oppression has been one of the most widespread and defining of modern experiences, and is a central component of post-colonialism, it seems a legitimate and fruitful one. But it should be stressed that, given the range of cultures from which our chosen dramatists come, it is not surprising that there is great diversity – as well as some common factors – in the historical processes of political and economic subjugation and in their cultural implications. The introductory chapter therefore explores some of these issues in more detail, to create a context for the particular responses to felt cultural oppression in the work of the dramatists discussed.

Though we have tried to place our playwrights in their cultural and artistic contexts, this is neither a comprehensive survey of drama and theatre in the Third or 'oppressed' World, nor even of the particular cultures to which they belong. A select bibliography offers guidance to where discussions not attempted here may be found – though much, it should be said, remains to be done. If what follows helps engender interest in and enthusiasm for the writers discussed, and stimulates thinking about drama's relation to the experiences of oppression and subjugation, it will have served its purpose.

The chapters on Badal Sircar and Girish Karnad were written by Chris Banfield; the rest of the book was written by Brian Crow.

Acknowledgements

We want to thank Dr Clare Lidbury, our colleague at Birmingham University, who read the first draft of this book and gave us useful comments as well as encouragement; Professor David Bradby, the general editor of the series in which the book appears, for his helpful criticisms and advice; and Juliette MacDonald for word processing the book with her usual efficiency and good humour.

Introduction

At its peak in the 1930s the British Empire covered almost a quarter of the world's land surface and embraced nearly a quarter of its population. It spanned every continent except Europe. If the United States had been long lost – and had already replaced Britain as the world's most powerful economic and political force – it still retained Canada and its Caribbean territories, Iraq and Egypt as its main colonies in the Middle East, large possessions in West, East and Southern Africa, a string of Asian colonies the jewel of which was India, and Australia and New Zealand. The nature and status of these constituents of empire were extremely varied. Canada, South Africa and Australasia, like the United States before them, had been settled by whites who had either decimated the indigenous peoples in their push for territorial expansion and their desire to reproduce European society, or ruthlessly exploited and controlled them: these white 'dominions' had already been granted 'responsible' government under the Crown. Britain's main Arab colonies were acquired as part of the colonial redivision after the First World War, and were soon to be granted their political if not entirely their economic independence (Iraq in 1932, Egypt in 1936). The tropical colonies of the Caribbean, Africa and Asia, except for the very special case of India, were ruled by governors and colonial officials without any prospect of the natives participating in government, at least within the foreseeable future. India was different for several reasons, not least the sheer size of the country and its population and the fact that it was already a highly developed military empire before the British arrived. The overwhelming pressures of Indian nationalism, combined with the Second World War, were to ensure the granting of independence in 1947.

The non-European peoples contained within this vast empire had little or nothing in common except their subjection. But even the forms of subjection varied widely, reflecting the variety of motives behind particular acts of colonization and the nature of the indigenous cultures colonized. If, in Australia, the invasion of white settlers often entailed the genocide of the Aboriginal population, or, as in South Africa, the ruthless economic exploitation and social control of the native peoples (culminating in the Nationalist government's official policy of apartheid from 1948), in India or Nigeria the everyday lives of most peasants remained more or less untouched by colonial subjection. And it was a different story again for those descendants of the vast number of Africans who were enslaved and shipped off to the Caribbean, or – outside the British Empire – to Brazil and the plantations of the southern United States. Nominally free men and women in the world's largest democratic republic, black Americans had to confront widespread racial discrimination, severe economic disadvantage, and the traumatic social and cultural disruptions of forced migration (a double migration in the case of those who sought a better life in the North).

Subordinated people experienced their domination differently even within the same society. The pain of humiliated subjugation might have been of more or less equal intensity for, say, the educated young black American schoolteacher or small-scale businessman, with aspirations to live like the white lower middle class, and the illiterate emigrant sharecropper from the South struggling to survive at the bottom of the heap in a Northern ghetto, but the context and psychological impact of that humiliation were likely to be very different. If, in colonial West Africa or India, close proximity to white authority figures, and the desire to 'improve oneself' could lead to outward – and sometimes internalized – deference on the part of 'white-collar' natives, the same was unlikely to be the case for the majority, whose contact with the white instruments of their colonial subjection was in any case often minimal. Apart from the humiliations enforced by the colour bar or petty apartheid the experience of colonial oppression was, for the masses, more likely to be blatantly economic and social, involving exploitation of their labour and disregard for what they might regard as their basic human rights, than subtly psychological.

A paradox, then, of the native experience of colonial (or, in the case of the black American, a sort of quasi-colonial) domination and oppression is that it was often not the poorest and most exploited but the more educated and relatively more privileged, those having closer contact with the agents of colonial domination, who felt most keenly the psychological and cultural impact of their subjugation. The classic studies of this syndrome are those by the Antillean psychiatrist Frantz Fanon, who identified what he calls 'a massive psycho-existential complex' in the relations between the coloured colonized and white colonialists, involving 'an existential deviation' forced on its victims by white civilization and European culture.

Central to Fanon's thinking is Hegel's perception of *recognition* as the basis of self-consciousness and of human relationship: 'Self-consciousness exists *in itself* and *for itself*, in that and by the fact that it exists for another self-consciousness; that is to say, it is only by being acknowledged or recognized.'[1] In this world of 'reciprocal recognitions' every individual requires the recognition of the other so as to win what Fanon calls 'the certainty of oneself'. We all, in other words, experience our being through others. What has happened, in the historical relations between whites and blacks, is that because of its belief in its racial superiority, associated with the economic and military dominance of colonialism, the white race has disrupted the reciprocity of this fundamental process of recognition. The black person looks for the human recognition accorded him by the other; but when the other is white, that acknowledgement is withheld, and the black is deprived of his 'certainty of himself'. So the black man 'makes himself abnormal'; and the white 'is at once the perpetrator and the victim of a delusion'.[2]

In this process of mutual recognition and cultural relationship language is crucial. In chapter one of *Black Skin, White Masks*,

---

[1] Hegel, *The Phenomenology of Mind*, quoted in Frantz Fanon, *Black Skin, White Masks*, London: Pluto Press, 1986, p. 216.

[2] *Ibid.*, p. 225.

entitled 'The Negro And Language', Fanon declares that 'to speak is to exist absolutely for the other'.[3] The act of communication through speech implies the agreement, by the speaker, to be at least for that moment a subject who voluntarily functions as an object for the other. At the same time, to 'speak a language is to take on a world, a culture' (p.38). The problem, in Fanon's view, is that given the relations between black and white, the white other only recognizes the humanity of his black interlocutor to the extent that the latter has mastery of the 'white' language: 'The Negro of the Antilles will be proportionately whiter – that is, he will come closer to being a real human being – in direct ratio to his mastery of the French language'[4] – which is also the mastery of French culture. A European foreigner trying to communicate with a French person but ignorant of his or her language may cause frustration but will not be despised, since it is understood that that person has a language, a history, a culture of his or her own. Not so the black, who is credited with none of these attributes: he can only aspire to the status of an honorary Frenchman, to the extent that education gives him a language that endows him with at least the appearance of 'civilization'. Fanon notes that such attitudes have been accepted even by many blacks: the black immigrant to France changes his language and self-presentation, and is a different person when he returns home; the African black may pretend to be an Antillean, and the Antillean is annoyed when he is taken for an African, since it is thought that the latter is less 'civilized', less 'French', than the person from the Caribbean.

There were important cultural differences between British and French colonialism, with its 'assimilationist' policy of creating 'black Frenchmen', and Fanon is in any case careful to insist that his observations and conclusions are valid only for the francophone West Indies, his personal experience of which – along with his work for the Algerian national liberation movement – so deeply influenced his theories. Moreover, he recognizes that the form of cultural and racial alienation experienced by those educated persons like himself is 'of an almost intellectual character', and quite different from the experi-

---

[3] *Ibid.*, p. 17.
[4] *Ibid.*, p. 18.

ences of, say, a labourer, or a peasant in francophone West Africa or Indo-China. Nevertheless, Fanon asserts that 'the same behaviour patterns obtain in every race that has been subjected to coloniz-ation'.[5]

Fanon spoke with the authority both of personal experience and of his knowledge as a psychiatrist. Much that he wrote is echoed by other black writers and intellectuals, with quite different kinds of colonial or oppressed histories, when they comment on the psycho-logical and cultural phenomena of subjugation. For example the Nigerian playwright Wole Soyinka, whose work we shall consider later, has written of 'the fragmented and even distorted consciousness of the black people in the midst of a domineering culture'.[6] And the black American writer James Baldwin, in *The Fire Next Time*, writes eloquently of what he believes has been the characteristic experience of generations of black Americans:

> This past, the Negro's past, of rope, fire, torture, castration,
> infanticide, rape; death and humiliation, fear by day and night,
> fear as deep as the marrow of the bone; doubt that he was
> worthy of life, since everyone around him denied it; sorrow for
> his women, for his kinfolk, for his children, who needed his
> protection, and whom he could not protect; rage, hatred, and
> murder, hatred for white men so deep that it often turned
> against him, and his own, and made all love, all trust, all joy
> impossible – this past, this endless struggle to achieve and
> reveal and confirm a human identity, human authority, yet
> contains for all its horror, something very beautiful.[7]

Baldwin's evocation of the desire to confirm a vital sense of identity and self-worth is a need described by many writers whose cultural legacy is one of subjugation and oppression. It is the inevitable reaction to a social context in which an alien, white power calls the shots, has the power to define, to judge. It is evidently not a single, unitary experience, the same in all contexts. The desire for self-

[5] *Ibid.*, p. 25.

[6] Wole Soyinka, *Art, Dialogue and Outrage: Essays on Literature and Culture*, London: Methuen, 1993, p. 52.

[7] James Baldwin, *The Fire Next Time*, London: Penguin, 1964, p. 84.

validation, for a secure sense of identity, might involve a psychological internalization of a white 'ideal', and be expressed, like the conduct of Fanon's Antillean in France, as mimicry of white language, behaviour and attitudes. But this is an extreme type of reaction to subjugation, and as Baldwin points out, 'I do not know many Negroes who are eager to be "accepted" by white people, still less to be loved by them.'[8] A quite different kind of response to the need for a recognition of one's human worth may be resistance and self-assertion, and what Soyinka calls the 'quest for racial self-retrieval', the recovery of 'an authentic cultural existence'.[9] It is just such a sustained and strong resistance, the oppressed person's achievement of his or her own 'authority', which Baldwin identifies as the 'something very beautiful' contained in the struggle to achieve identity.

We must be cautious, even so, about assuming that all colonized or oppressed peoples have somehow 'lost' their 'identity'. Soyinka, for example, is scathing about the kind of modern African writer who 'even tried to give society something that the society had never lost – its identity'.[10] The exercise of oppressive power may have sought to impair – or at least had the effect of doing so – the sense of a unique cultural identity by eradicating it altogether, or by bastardizing it, or by marginalizing it to the point of impotence. Some subjugated peoples, the Australian Aborigines for example, have been so culturally devastated by white invasion that many of its members have virtually lost all connection with, and sustenance from, their cultural heritage. But in colonized societies with rich indigenous cultures (for example West Africa or India) that remained largely intact – whatever the colonialists may have wished or done – not only was cultural identity not lost, it has served as a potent weapon in the struggle for independence and liberation.

Similar caution is necessary about the issue of language in subordinated cultures, which as Fanon and others have shown is crucially related to the need for a secure cultural identity, and to the achievement of self-worth and self-determination. It is rather fashionable, in discussions of post-colonial literature and drama, to assert

---

[8] *Ibid.*, p. 27.

[9] Soyinka, *Art, Dialogue and Outrage*, pp. 86, 87.

[10] *Ibid.*, p. 17.

that colonial subjugation robbed indigenous writers of their own 'voices', reducing them to mimicry or silence. Only gradually, according to this line of thought, did post-colonial writers throw off their linguistic and cultural chains, re-appropriating the language of subjection and reforming it to become an authentic expression of their own experience. Though there are enough elements of truth in this account to make it persuasive, there are also serious omissions and distortions. It tends to ignore – perhaps because of linguistic ignorance – the remarkable range of literature and performance in indigenous languages that articulated criticism of and resistance to colonial rule and its characteristics. It also seems hard to square with a passage such as the following, from the Australian Aboriginal dramatist and poet Jack Davis's autobiography:

> I had always been interested in language, and found the English language and its history exciting to study. The hidden roots of English, in particular Latin and Greek, made the dictionary a constant source of fascination to me. Now that I was living among the Nyoongahs, that interest embraced the Nyoongah language.[11]

What Davis expresses here is his fascination both with English, in the case of the Aborigines the language of a particularly barbaric oppression, and with his own tribal language – with apparently no great distinction made between them, or sense of resentment against the 'alien' tongue.

Something equally surprising – at least if one thinks of post-colonial writers as 'silenced' by the language of colonial subjection – is expressed by the Indian playwright Badal Sircar, whose work will also be discussed later:

> To us, it [i.e. English] is not a neutral language. It is associated with the British imperialist rule over our country. By rights and by nature I should feel aversion to it. Yet this language has been more of a medium of my education than my own language –

[11] Jack Davis with Keith Chesson, *Jack Davis: a Life-Story*, Melbourne: Dent, 1988, p. 55.

and for me this language has been a window to the wide world. Hence, logically, I should be thankful to it. Another contradiction.[12]

And yet another is that in spite of Sircar's personally positive feelings about the 'imperialist' language (which still, paradoxically, provides the common language for educated Indians) his view is that it would be an entirely inappropriate language for his own theatre, and that his Bengali compositions resist completely successful translation into English.

These examples are not intended to demonstrate that post-colonial writers, whatever the (mainly Western) theorists may say, have been really quite comfortable with the inherited colonial language, but to suggest the real complexity of the language issue. If some, like Badal Sircar and of late the Kenyan playwright and novelist Ngugi wa Thiong'o, have renounced English as an artistic language and prefer to compose in their native tongues, others – such as Wole Soyinka and Derek Walcott – have preferred, whatever their sense of ambivalence about it, to write in the 'imperialist' language, forging distinctive and often strikingly powerful styles of English. Such choices have implications, of course, for the nature and extent of their audience: as Ngugi points out, 'the choice of a language already predetermines the answer to the most important question for producers of imaginative literature: For whom do I write? Who is my audience?'[13] And this in turn, as he insists, has implications for what they write about and what attitudes they take to their material. In any case, though the post-colonial dramatist can hardly avoid issues of language and the ambivalent and often contradictory feelings attached to them, what needs to be stressed is the richness with which they have created the linguistic means to render their and their people's experiences. Whether in their own indigenous languages, or in some inflection of the perhaps both loved and hated colonial tongue, it seems to be latter-day metropolitan arrogance – however well-meaning – to suppose that the native has ever been rendered

---

[12] Badal Sircar, unpublished manuscript, 1988.

[13] Ngugi wa Thiong'o, *Writers in Politics*, London: Heinemann, 1981, pp. 53–4.

mute. Post-colonial writers and artists, like ordinary people, seem always to have been able to communicate what they wished to their chosen audiences.

If there have been linguistic traps that the post-colonial dramatist has been forced to negotiate, there have also been issues of class, ethnicity and nationality that could not be avoided. The general context informing these debates concerning identity and language is the desire for cultural self-determination and an integrated identity, what Soyinka has called 'cultural certitude', and the attempt to achieve it through a kind of cultural 'return to roots'. This is expressed in different ways by different writers, but they seem to have something like the same thing in mind. Ngugi wa Thiong'o, for instance, speaks of the fundamental aim of 'restoring the African personality to its true human creative potentialities in history', involving 'a return to the roots of our being', which seems to have much in common with Soyinka's call for the 'evocation of an authentic tradition in the cause of society's transformation process', which he also sees as a 'self-retrieval' or 'cultural recollection'. For Derek Walcott this process seems to involve the artist, and specifically the actor, in a 'return through a darkness whose terminus is amnesia' if West Indian theatre is ever to express the authentic cultural being of its people: 'For imagination and body to move with original instinct,we must begin again from the bush. That return journey, with all its horror of rediscovery, means the annihilation of what is known.'[14] And the idea is evidently as important in contemporary Indian theatre as it is amongst writers of Africa and the black diaspora: during the 1988 national drama festival in New Delhi a 'Theatre of Roots' round-table was convened to discuss the progress of a scheme first implemented some four years earlier.

The common impulse to a 'return to roots' has forced many writers to confront other dilemmas relating to race, class and nationhood. K. S. Kothari, one of the moving spirits behind the 'theatre of roots' movement in India, has spoken of 'both the need and search for that indefinable quality called 'Indianness' in Indian

[14] Derek Walcott, 'What the Twilight Says: An Overture' in *Dream on Monkey Mountain and Other Plays*, New York: Farrar, Straus & Giroux, 1986, pp. 25–6.

theatre'.[15] But what can such 'Indianness' be, in a nation made up of several major religions, so many different classes and social groups, so many different peoples and languages, so many and diverse regional interests? Again, Soyinka and Ngugi, themselves writing from apparently differing political positions, have articulated the need to restore the African cultural personality as a major element of social development, but what is it that must be restored? Nigeria and Kenya, as national entities, are the creations of British imperialism, the forcible amalgamations of different peoples with different languages and often widely diverse cultures. In their histories since independence intense class and factional conflicts, involving widely differing economic interests, standards of living and ideologies, have developed within the fragile arena of the nation-state. Can there really be a 'Nigerianness' or a 'Kenyanness', or simply an 'African-ness', which somehow transcends all these factors?

The belief that there are indeed such essences has sometimes led to what Edward Said calls 'nativism' – phenomena, such as the negritude movement, which conjure up potent images of what a people or community was supposed to be before colonialism. As Said points out, such imagery is ahistorical, concerned more with 'the metaphysics of essences' than with any ascertainable historical realities. This kind of 'return', in cultural terms, is often associated with some mood or other of nostalgia, and the exaltation of what Soyinka scornfully calls 'the resuscitated splendours of the past' and Derek Walcott 'a schizophrenic daydream of an Eden' that existed before exile. Politically, it may be the ideological banner waved by reactionary nationalism, or the tattered cloak that conceals the nakedness of corrupt, incompetent and exploitative politicians.

But there is evidently another altogether more positive side to the idea of a cultural 'return'. This has to do with the urgent need of subjugated peoples, as an essential part of the process of decoloniz-ation, to recuperate their own histories, their own social and cultural traditions, their own narratives and discourses – all in the service, not of a myth of racial essence, but of what Said describes, citing Fanon,

---

[15]   K. S. Kothari, ' "Theatre of Roots", Encounter with Tradition', *TDR*, 33:4 (T124).

as a 'liberation' that is also 'a transformation of social consciousness beyond national consciousness'.[16] Such an encounter with the real past and with real traditions may for many have to include, as James Baldwin points out, the confronting of horror, anguish and humiliation. It is of course bound to bring tensions and contradictions to the surface, and to provoke difficult questions. It is likely to force, say, a Nigerian or Indian dramatist to consider – if he or she is a Yoruba or a Gujerati drawing on specific cultural materials from his or her particular ethnic well – how effectively he may hope to recuperate and communicate a collective 'self-apprehension' for his *national* audience. Or to ponder, with Soyinka, on whether the new African nations (or, one might add, the subcontinent of India) 'may not actually possess a unified culture', and to debate his ambivalent conclusion that 'we cannot afford to agonise unnecessarily over the suspicion'.[17] But such a 'return to roots' will be a creative and healthy process if it rediscovers and reinterprets what that same writer calls 'those elements which render a society unique in its own being, with a potential for its progressive transformation',[18] rather than an ideologically convenient mythology.

For the post-colonial playwright theatre has meant both traditional indigenous performance – which has often had to be rediscovered and reinvented – and the theatre that the colonists brought with them from the metropolitan power, usually in particularly impoverished and amateur forms. In the latter case, its penetration was almost entirely restricted to urban areas, sometimes only to the larger, more 'metropolitan' cities. Its audiences, at least outside elite educational institutions, were mainly white colonists and the more 'culture conscious' of the indigenous bourgeoisie. Its legacy was the imposition of the proscenium arch stage, the 'well-made' realist play, and, in the British Empire, Shakespeare.

It is easy to see the absurdity of an audience sweating its way through a stilted performance of *A Midsummer Night's Dream* or

---

[16] Edward Said, *Culture and Imperialism*, London: Chatto & Windus, 1993, p. 278.

[17] Soyinka, *Art, Dialogue and Outrage*, pp. 138–39.

[18] *Ibid.*, p.183

An Inspector Calls in an ill-equipped colonial hall on a hot tropical night in Africa or India, especially when all around, unknown or unacknowledged, were indigenous theatrical riches that the Western avant-garde would one day set out on cultural safaris to 'discover'. Less obvious is the likelihood that such performances, inadequate as they may have been, were often windows to new and exciting artistic worlds for prospective young dramatists who were fascinated by Shakespeare's language, by the psychological insights of an Ibsen or a Priestley, and by the wonders – however limited in such settings – wrought by modern stage technology. So yet another contradiction: metropolitan theatre as imposition and at the same time as catalyst; as alien import and as access to new experience that was not all alien since at its best and most interesting it spoke to some at least of our putative young dramatists' experiences. And if, like a Soyinka or a Sircar, one then went to the metropole, to witness and even participate in the theatrical experiments being conducted – we are speaking now of the 1960s – at theatres such as the Royal Court in London or by companies such as the Living Theatre in America, then the contradictions could only be heightened – especially when the young post-colonial dramatist's excited contact was with Western practitioners who, ironically, were drawing much of their inspiration from their (usually highly selective) acquaintance with 'colonial' theatre.

If such Western influences have been formative for young post-colonial playwrights, so has been the desire, usually once a certain artistic maturity has been achieved, to reacquaint (or acquaint) themselves with their indigenous theatrical and perform-ance traditions. In contrast with the Western tradition of realist drama and acting, these traditional modes of performance are usually stylized, often incorporate dance, music and song, and operate from an oral rather than a literary base. In relation to the dramatists discussed here, they embrace a remarkable range, including Indian classical and folk forms, West African and Caribbean storytelling performance, Yoruba ritual dramas performed in honour of Ogun and other deities, Aboriginal storytelling and corroborees, and preaching in black American churches.

The rediscovery (or, sometimes, discovery) of indigenous

performance traditions has often served to emphasize the limitations of Western realism in terms both of writing and performance. For Badal Sircar and Girish Karnad, for example, it has offered a means of escape from the physical constraints of the proscenium arch stage, with its distinctive and for them alien separation of the worlds of stage and audience. As Suresh Awasthi has pointed out, the first proscenium arch theatres built in Bombay and Calcutta in the 1860s radically changed the traditional character of Indian theatrical space, which had included an intimate, interactive relationship between spectators and actors and the capacity to watch performances from different angles and levels, allowing a constantly changing perception of the action. As we shall see, however, the 'return' to traditional theatre has not entailed an acceptance, by either Sircar or Karnad, of the traditional values associated with it. As Karnad has pointed out, in the hands of a playwright with a dissenting political agenda and a contemporary sensibility[19] the forms of folk theatre can be used for critical and subversive ends.

But the post-colonial dramatist's reversion to native traditions of performance has done more than provide him or her with a rich source of stylistic or dramaturgical conventions and devices. We said earlier that traditional theatre also constitutes one of the main artistic means of cultural recuperation generally; and in this respect the rediscovery of the indigenous traditions allows the dramatist to tap into the current that energized the cultural past. The full significance that such an engagement may have is revealed by Wole Soyinka's reflections on the 'drama of the gods' in his *Myth, Literature and the African World*. For Soyinka, the preservation of his society's awareness of its interrelation with the natural and spiritual orders requires the enactment of communal ritual drama in which the protagonist-actor relives the god Ogun's original, redemptive journey across the 'dark continuum of transition' connecting the 'worlds' of the living, the ancestors and the unborn. Through his immersion in the 'primal reality' of the drama, the ritual actor performs a vital function for the community; 'he is enabled empathically to transmit its essence to the choric participants of the

---

[19] See chapter 7 below.

rites'[20] and thus to energize and strengthen them. In spite of 'ritual-istic earthing' – provided by the surrounding participant-audience as well as sacrifices and propitiations – the ritual protagonist, like Ogun, risks personal destruction, presumably in the form of psychic dis-integration, as he makes his journey across the abyss of transition. The stage of ritual drama, then, is not a place of mimetic represent-ation, but the dangerous arena of spiritual confrontation and trans-formation. By comparison, literary-based tragic drama is a rather pale shadow – a 'mundane reflection' in Soyinka's phrase – of this ritual performance. But it is nevertheless the experience of confrontation and integration with cosmic forces, conducted on behalf of an entire community, that Soyinka seeks to recreate.

For Derek Walcott, too, traditional performance is a source of more than technical inspiration. If, in his view, the state has politicized and commercialized 'folk' art for its own ends, it has not succeeded in colonizing the genuine folk imagination, and he has beautifully evoked its world and its significance for the making of theatre:

> And there were vampires, witches, gardeurs, masseurs (usually a fat black foreign-smelling blackness, with gold-rimmed spectacles), not to mention the country where the night withheld a whole, unstarred mythology of flaming, shed skins. Best of all, in the lamplit doorway at the creaking hour, the stories sung by old Sidone, a strange croaking of Christian and African songs . . . They sang of children lost in the middle of a forest, where the leaves' ears pricked at the rustling of devils, and one did not know if to weep for the first two brothers of every legend, one strong, the other foolish.[21]

The oral folk tradition has profoundly influenced his own and West Indian theatre, Walcott observes, primarily by communicating its symmetry, its universal sense of triadic structure:

---

[20] Wole Soyinka, *Myth, Literature and the African World*, Cambridge: Cambridge University Press, 1976, p. 33.
[21] Walcott, 'What the Twilight Says', pp. 23–4.

It kept the same digital rhythm of three movements, three acts,
three moral revelations, whether it was the tale of three sons or
three bears, whether it ended in tragedy or happily ever after.
It has sprung from hearthside or lamplit hut-door in an age
when the night outside was a force, inimical, infested with
devils, wood-demons, a country for the journey of the soul, and
any child who has heard its symmetry chanted would want to
retell it when he was his own story-teller, with the same respect
for its shape.[22]

If the folk-tale performance offers a formal model for the Caribbean
playwright it has also, at least for Walcott, been a larger cultural
inspiration – 'a country for the journey of the soul'.

Extraordinary as it would have seemed at the peak of its power in the
1930s, the British Empire had virtually ceased to exist by the early
1960s. The first wave of decolonization, mainly in the Middle East
and South East Asia, occurred in the late 1940s, soon after – and
partly because of – the Second World War. The second wave began in
1956, with the first tropical African country, Ghana (formerly the
Gold Coast), gaining its independence in 1957. By 1963 most of the
former British colonies in Africa were independent, as also were
Jamaica, Trinidad and Tobago.

But for all the high hopes of the radical nationalists, who had
achieved independence so quickly and in many (but not all) cases
painlessly, their freedom from colonial subjection did not mean the
end of domination *per se*. If colonialism involved the direct political
and economic control of a subject territory, in the period of neo-
colonialism since independence control has typically been exercised
indirectly, by means variously of unequal trade relations, indebted-
ness, and the threat (and sometimes the reality) of military or
economic force. In this new age of imperialism the two great imperial
powers have been the USA and, until its recent demise, the USSR.

The forms of subordination prevailing until very recently in
the 'client' states of the Eastern Bloc and in the peripheral capitalist
countries of the Third World were very different (and diverse even

[22] *Ibid.*, p. 24.

amongst themselves), but one feature in common has been the important role in both of cultural manipulation in supporting political and economic subjugation. An indication of this, in Eastern Europe, is paradoxically suggested by the crucial roles played by cultural forces and institutions in the overthrow of the ruling communist governments – for example, the churches in the German Democratic Republic and the liberal progressives, many of them associated with the arts and media, clustered around the playwright-president Vaclav Havel in the Civic Forum movement, in what used to be Czechoslovakia. For the Kenyan writer and political dissident Ngugi wa Thiong'o, cultural imperialism 'becomes the major agency of control during neocolonialism'[23] and 'the cultural and the psychological aspects of imperialism become even more important as instruments of mental and spiritual coercion'.[24] What Ngugi has in mind is effective Western (primarily American) control of news and information, of the images disseminated on television, video, film and radio, of book and magazine publishing, and even of higher and more specialized forms of education and training.

Nominal independence, then – at least for those who agree with Ngugi and other radical critics of the contemporary world order – is no guarantee of cultural self-determination. The struggle goes on, in a particularly intense form, for the definition and assertion of an authentic rather than an imposed identity, by those who have long been subjugated and subordinated. As Edward Said points out, 'the assertion of identity is by no means a mere ceremonial matter' in the contemporary world.[25] And indeed, given the many failures of democracy and development as well as the blatant corruption and power seeking in the post-colonial nations, their writers and intellectuals can no longer confidently evoke the images and emotions that fuelled the earlier national independence movements. In some cases these have calcified or been distorted into reactionary political and cultural 'returns', to roots identified in religious terms (for example, as fundamentalist Islam or Hinduism) or as some kind of ethnic 'essence'.

[23] Ngugi wa Thiong'o, *Writers in Politics*, p. 5.
[24] Ngugi wa Thiong'o, *Moving the Centre*, London: James Currey, 1993, p. 52.
[25] Said, *Culture and Imperialism*, p.42.

In such post- but neocolonial contexts dramatists have created theatre for a variety of urgent cultural functions. They have often been concerned to use the stage to define and affirm their people's cultural 'personality' – in the face of continuing cultural, economic and political subjugation – by recovering the past, freed from the biases of metropolitan or mainstream history. They have often sought to expose the forces that still obstruct liberation, whether these be, for blacks in America, Australia or South Africa, the oppressions of dominant white society or the mendacity of ruling indigenous elites, or – and these are sometimes the most potent antagonists, and the most difficult to confront – attitudes and behaviour ingrained within the oppressed themselves. They have sometimes looked inward, questioning the nature, status and effect of art and the artist in their societies. And they have also, at their finest, intimated where might be found the sources of cultural renewal – for culture is a continuing process of decay and renewal – where one might at least begin the journey towards the country of the soul.

Derek Walcott and a Caribbean theatre of revelation

When Frantz Fanon made his remarkable analysis of the psycho-existential nature of relations between dominators and dominated under colonialism, he admitted that he was writing from the specific perspective of an educated Antillean, and that therefore 'my observations and my conclusions are valid only for the Antilles'.[1] But at the risk of self-contradiction he also insisted, a little later in the same work, that 'the same behaviour patterns obtain in every race that has been subjected to colonization'.[2] It may be that though the same behaviour patterns do indeed apply more or less universally, they may be more in evidence in, and more acutely relevant to, certain conditions of subjection than to others. There is at least the possibility that Fanon's insights into the problematic complexities of interpersonal relations, in a racist and colonial context, spring not just from his particular vocational interests as a psychiatrist but derive, more generally, from the distinctive character of colonial forms of domination in the Caribbean. Marked by its distinctive history of plantation slavery and ethnic multiplicity (European and African, but also Indian and Chinese), and the particular kinds of interpersonal racial interaction associated with that history, it may be that there has tended to be an especially intense psychological dimension to the Caribbean experience of domination that has not been felt, at least not in such an acute form, in some other colonial and neocolonial contexts.

Fanon notes, with wry humour, some of the nuances of racial

---

[1] Frantz Fanon, *Black Skin, White Masks*, p. 16.
[2] *Ibid.*, p. 25.

discrimination between Antillean blacks themselves, and between Antilleans and other blacks from francophone Africa. Many commentators have observed the significance attached to gradations of skin colour in the West Indies, even in the post-independence era. And, in what seems to be a related phenomenon, several West Indian writers, including V. S. Naipaul and the subject of this discussion, Derek Walcott, have commented on another common Caribbean psycho-cultural characteristic, at least among some of the educated black elite – the desolating sense that nothing genuinely original or worthwhile could be created on these islands, that its inhabitants in general and, alas, its artists in particular, have been doomed to the sterile mimicry of others, caught – and lost – as they have been between their originating cultures (African but also Indian and to some extent Chinese) and the metropolitan colonial or neocolonial societies (Britain, France, America).

In Walcott's case it is easy to see that such a perception might well be reinforced by his twenty-year struggle to establish a professional theatre company in Trinidad – by far the most sustained attempt to do so – which ended in failure and disillusionment. A similar conviction may also be strengthened, at least for those seeking artistically serious but commercially viable theatre in the West Indies, by the relative lack of popular enthusiasm for theatre in general compared with other forms of entertainment such as music and sport. When theatre does exercise a popular appeal, it is mainly because of its exploitation of comedy and sentiment. Nor can it be said that there has been steady progress towards a more satisfactory and hopeful state of artistic affairs. Emigration has taken away many of the Caribbean's brightest and best, traditionally to Europe but more recently to North America; while tourism, the American mass media and the 'glamorous' images of the American way of life have had a deep and debilitating effect on West Indian culture and self-identity.

This persistent and somewhat despondent sense of West Indian cultural mediocrity, at least as far as 'serious' theatre is concerned, has to be set next to the extraordinary vitality of its popular music, song and dance, as well as the vigour of its prose fiction and poetry. Over the years a debate has developed about the relationship between 'low' and 'high' theatrical forms and about what, if anything, in the former might offer a basis for the growth of a popularly based but artistically serious drama. The most significant of the perceived growth-points for a vital but exploratory Caribbean theatre is Trinidadian Carnival (though some other islands have now adopted it, partly for touristic reasons), which grew out of the African slaves' adaptation of carnival entertainment originally imported by whites from Europe. The veteran West Indian scholar and playwright Errol Hill argues in his authoritative study of Trinidadian Carnival that it can form the basis of a 'national theatre'; and Hill has tried, as have others, to put his own prescription into practice, for example in *Man Better Man*, which incorporates carnivalesque elements of music, song and dance. Whether such an evolution is possible, or even desirable, remains debatable; what is clear, thus far, is that in spite of awareness of, and occasional individual attempts to exploit, the theatrical resources of Carnival and other traditional forms such as spirit-possession performances, the Papa Diable masquerade, the Crop-Over and the Jonkonnu, these have in general played little if any major role in the development of West Indian theatre forms. By far the most popular form is in fact comedy, in guises little different in terms of theatrical conventions from those found in many other cultures.

More than any particular performance mode, it is the folk imagination that has deeply influenced and helped shape West Indian theatre, both directly through its borrowing of characters, stories and images from the rich oral tradition and, more pervasively, through its inheritance of the imaginative world of the folk-tale. Though the traditional folk-tale and its performance traditions are evident in many West Indian plays, nowhere have they been more richly exploited than in the drama of Derek Walcott, or more beautifully evoked than in his memoir-cum-critical essay, 'What The Twilight Says: An Overture' (see introduction, pp. 9–11). Walcott is without doubt the major – indeed the only major – dramatist that the Caribbean has so far produced. Describing himself as a 'mongrel', a 'neither proud nor ashamed bastard', Walcott has had a long and pioneering career in West Indian and especially Trinidadian theatre, in the course of which he has been artistically faithful to his self-proclaimed 'mongrelism', constantly experimenting with a range of theatrical form, genre and theme. Exploiting the narrative and formal possibilities of folk-tale and legend in such plays of the 1950s and sixties as *Ti-Jean and His Brothers* and *Dream on Monkey Mountain*, Walcott has subsequently extended his range to include versions of European classics (*The Joker of Seville* and, more recently, his dramatized adaptation of Homer's *Odyssey* for the Royal Shakespeare Company), tragi-comedy (*Remembrance*), a musical about Rastafarianism (*O Babylon!*), comedy and farce (*Pantomime, Beef, no Chicken*), and drama in which the distinctive lyricism of his poetic language is combined with the urgent exploration of the tensions of West Indian politics, culture and art (*The Last Carnival, A Branch of the Blue Nile*).

Walcott no doubt includes himself in the category of writer he calls 'the mulatto of style', whose efforts to purify the language of the tribe inevitably invite accusations of treachery, assimilation, pretentiousness and 'playing white'.[3] The diversity of his writing, even if we consider only his work for the stage, indicates the numerous attempts to absorb both his inheritances, African and European (Ashanti and Warwickshire, to be exact) – to find a language, a style, a form that can authentically express West Indian reality without mimicry of either. Walcott has written powerfully of the forms that cultural mimicry may take, and of the bonds that the West Indian artist must break to release him- or herself from such servitude. The quest for liberation from the pervasive sense of colonial subordination and inauthenticity, the search for 'a dialect which has the force of revelation', has been the main impulse shaping the variety of formal experiments he has undertaken as a playwright. It has also influenced the content of his dramatic writing, giving it a remarkable degree of thematic continuity. Underlying Walcott's drama over many years has been a constant theme, expressed through his preoccupation with characters who have a fundamental quarrel with West Indian reality.

In his earliest published plays this hostility is presented as elemental, inscribed in the harshness of the natural environment and in the

---

[3] Derek Walcott, 'What the Twilight Says: An Overture', p. 9.

even harsher lineaments of human nature. The struggle here is against the indifferent cruelty of the sea from which Afa and the other fishermen of *The Sea at Dauphin* are doomed to seek their liveli-hoods; or against the diabolical evil of the white planter who destroys Ti-Jean's two brothers before he is finally mastered by the young man's cunning stratagem against oppression; or, as in *Malcochon, or The Six in the Rain*, it is presented as the savagery of the human beast, finally redeemed, even as he is murdered, by the mad old outcast Chantal.

In these early plays Walcott achieves, for Caribbean theatre, qualities associated in European drama with Synge and Lorca. The elemental experience of the peasant characters is presented in an already assured combination of folk-tale structure, with its universal symmetry ('the one armature from Br'er Anancy to King Lear'), and the local, poetic force of peasant dialect. Inspired by the folk stories he heard sung or told in his youth, Walcott brings his narratives to theatrical life through such devices as *conteurs*, on-stage musicians, song and dance, choruses and masks. The dramatic world thus created achieves, in theatrical terms, something of that timeless, legendary quality associated with the folk-tale in all cultures. At its finest, in *Dream on Monkey Mountain* (1967), this creative exploit-ation of folk narrative in the theatre succeeds in forging a new version of the expressionistic, psychological dream play that can evoke not only an individual's anguished consciousness but the dramatist's complex sense of the condition of his people.

Though the possibilities of the folk tradition have provided one theatrical model for Walcott's writing, he has also experimented with formal possibilities offered by the Euro-American tradition. As a rule, where the quarrel with West Indian reality involves peasant or working-class characters struggling against their natural or social environment, sometimes in the process invoking a vision of Africa as their salvation, Walcott's form is popular and often modelled on folk story. But when the dramatic conflict is generated by or associated with the tension between 'West Indianness' and the characters' relation to white, European culture, his use of dramatic form is recognizably 'Western' and contemporary.

Several of the plays in this latter category specifically explore the dilemmas of the artist in a subordinated culture, featuring characters whose personal and artistic identities are markedly affected by the tensions they experience between their West Indianness and the cultural power of the metropolis, whether this be identified with Paris, London or New York.

In *Remembrance* (1977) the artist is a minor Trinidadian writer and schoolteacher, Albert Perez Jordan, whose abiding love has been for the English language of Britain and its traditional literature. Not a great deal that's evidently or conclusively 'dramatic' happens in the play. In the course of an interview with a young reporter from the local newspaper, Jordan's reminiscences blend with the words of his stories and scenes from the past on which they were based. In the first story, the satirical 'Barrley and the Roof', Jordan's son Frederick, an aspiring artist, paints the stars and stripes on the roof of the family home, but refuses to sell it to an American art collector, Barrley, much to his father's disgust. In the second, 'My War Effort', Jordan's story (set in Trinidad during the Second World War), blends into a flashback of his relationship with his English boss at the information office, a Miss Esther Trout (Hope in the fiction), whom he courts like a black Englishman – or rather a parody of an Englishman – quoting *Henry V* and playing the gallant officer and gentleman as he proposes marriage to her. Then, at lunch one day, she accepts, to be greeted by Jordan's silence and his quick exit to the men's room:

> I went to the men's room for twenty years. . . . A mortal error.
> To stay within the boundaries of my race and not cross over,
> even for love. Esther! I'll never look upon her like again. Since
> then I have been a mind without a country. From that day
> onward I have always known my place. The end. (p. 46)

But a few moments later Albert does find himself looking upon her like again, or so he persuades himself, in the person of Anna Herschel, a young American drifter with a baby. She stays for a while, Albert reliving his memories of Esther and encouraging his son to leave Trinidad and go off with her. But in spite of their affection for each other she leaves alone, and Frederick resolves to stay on the island and continue painting. Jordan is left alone, quoting Gray's *Elegy* as

he hears in memory the voices of the generations of children he has
taught.

There are dramatic weaknesses in *Remembrance*, especially in
its second act: the arrival and departure of Anna are both implausible,
and her relationships with Jordan and Frederick are too sketchy to be
completely interesting, or to develop effectively the parallel with
Esther. There are references throughout to another son killed during
Black Power riots seven years previously, whose grave Jordan has
never visited on his day of remembrance; but the character's inability
to cope with the tragedy of his death seems to extend into Walcott's
dramatic treatment, which never satisfactorily integrates its emotional significance into the theme of remembrance.

The play works best when it evokes with pathos and humour
the mixture of memory, desire and regret, of fiction and the reality on
which it is based, in Jordan's mind. It captures both the poignancy
and absurdity of an older West Indian's love for and cowardice
towards a British culture that has formed him but to which he can
never belong, and which makes him psychologically a misfit everywhere, even in his own society. At one point Esther responds to
Jordan's literary English with 'Your accent is almost flawless, Mr
Jordan. When are you going to be yourself?' The answer seems to be
never: for all his solidity as a dramatic character, Jordan is a portrait
of the artist as a failure in life and art, both fractured by his inability
to forge an authentic identity as a black Trinidadian.

In two of his plays, *Pantomime* (1978) and *A Branch of the
Blue Nile* (1983), Walcott's portrait of the post-colonial artist focuses
specifically on actors and the theatre. *Pantomime* is a two-hander in
which a former actor from England, Harry Trewe, tries to interest his
Trinidadian factotum, Jackson Phillip, a retired calypsonian, in
putting together a show to entertain the guests at his none too
successful guest house on Tobago. Harry's idea is for them to do
sketches based on *Robinson Crusoe*, but with the roles reversed to
give the audience a bit of innocuously light satirical entertainment.
Jackson thinks the idea 'is shit' but eventually begins to improvise
on it to try to demonstrate to his boss its historical implications.
Through role-play he shows Harry how, if the roles were really
reversed, he would have to play the servant for three hundred years,

performing the pantomime of being the white man's shadow. The white man smiles at his servant 'as a child does smile at his shadow's helpless obedience', but

> after a while the child does get frighten of the shadow he make. He say to himself, That is too much obedience, I better hads stop. But the shadow don't stop, no matter if the child stop playing that pantomime, and the shadow does follow the child everywhere.... He cannot get rid of it, no matter what, and that is the power and black magic of the shadow, boss, bwana, effendi, bacra, sahib, until it is the shadow that start dominating the child, it is the servant that start dominating the master. (p. 113)

Harry's enthusiasm for his own idea dwindles as Jackson warms to his improvisation, inventing a new language that his servant will have to learn and forcing his discomfited boss to play the ignominious roles of a large seabird and a goat, which the black Crusoe will kill and skin to make a parasol and hat. When Harry announces that he's 'had enough of this farce' and wants Jackson to stop, he's told that this is the story of history itself: 'This moment that we are now acting here is the history of imperialism; it's nothing less than that. And I don't think that I can – should – concede my getting into a part halfway and abandoning things, just because you, as my superior, give me orders. People become independent' (p. 125).

What Harry and Jackson come to acknowledge is that they are both socially miscast. As Jackson says: 'You see, two of we both acting a role here we ain't really believe in, you know. I ent think you strong enough to give people orders, and I *know* I ain't the kind who like taking *them*. So both of we doesn't have to *improvise* so much as *exaggerate*. We faking, faking all the time' (p. 138).

When they resume their role-playing in act two it is with a new intent, the servant seeking to make a reformed man of his lonely, empty boss. As Jackson role-plays Harry's wife the Englishman's bitterness and aggression towards her are revealed and apparently exorcised through the emotion aroused. Harry achieves a new understanding: 'An angel passes through a house and leaves no imprint of his shadow on its wall. A man's life slowly changes and he does not understand the change. Things like this have happened before, and they can happen again' (p. 169). And Jackson also makes a decision as a result of the day's activity. He 'benignly' resigns his present job to return to his true calling: 'Caiso is my true work, caiso is my true life' (p. 170). They prepare to do a show together for the new season's guests, which they will call 'Pantomime'.

Harry's and Jackson's agreement to collaborate in a theatrical venture, in however modest a way, at the end of *Pantomime* coincides with their achievement of a new personal understanding. Walcott's play suggests that theatre may not only offer insight into social and cultural relations – in this case between black and white, colonized and colonizer – but actively bring about new awareness, and hence new relationships, through the active power of role-play. It is not, as in *Remembrance*, the black product of colonialism who suffers the crisis: Jackson is not the sort of character who would have heard of Frantz Fanon, but in his down-to-earth way he understands very clearly the historical mechanism of his race's oppression. It is the expatriate Englishman Harry Trewe who has the crisis of identity and purpose, and who is brought through his employee's powers of role-play to a resolution that seems to be intended as both personal and social.

The power of the actor and performance is the subject of *A Branch of the Blue Nile* (1983), Walcott's portrait of the artistic and personal relationships of members of a contemporary West Indian theatre company. The company and the play centre around Sheila, a semi-professional black Trinidadian actress, who in the course of rehearsing the role of Cleopatra in Shakespeare's play discovers the special, magical truth of the actress's complete absorption in, and control of, her art. She refers to this experience in religious terms, as being a state of 'grace', and such is its effect on her that she is led to renounce the theatre for religion proper, in the form of a branch of the Adventist Church. Another member of the company, the playwright Chris, Sheila's lover, prophecies that this event in their rehearsal will have a profound but divisive effect on them all: 'We have found the truth. At least some part of it. And you know what go happen? It go split us up. You doubt me? Talk the truth. Anybody doubt me?' (p. 223). He is right. By the end Chris himself is living in Barbados with his English wife, having written a play about the company. Harvey, their white West Indian director, has returned to England to die, Marylin has gone off to seek fame and fortune in the States, and Gavin, who has already tried his luck there and come back disillusioned because of the professional racism he encountered, is teaching acting in Jamaica. Only Sheila herself, of the original company, stands in the dark, silent theatre, having turned away from the Church to follow her true vocation as an actor.

Though the characters' lives are decisively altered in the course of it, *A Branch of the Blue Nile* is like *Pantomime* in having very little actually happening in it, apart from people speaking to each other. Their conversations revolve obsessively around a number of related topics: the nature and value of theatre in a post-colonial society such as Trinidad's; the post-colonial theatre practitioner's experience of working in metropolitan countries; and most pervasively of all the relation of personal experience, and the 'truth' it may have, to the work of the performer.

The main authorial statement about this is made at the end of the play, not by one of the main characters but by the crazed yet visionary ex-performer Phil, when he joins Sheila in the empty theatre where he sometimes seeks shelter:

> Oh, God, a actor is a holy thing. A sacred thing. Then, when it so quiet that one cough sound like thunder, and you know you have them where you want them, is not you anymore but the gift, the gift. And you know the gift ain't yours but something God lend you for a lickle while. Even in this country. Even here. (p. 312)

Inspired by Harvey's method of intensive, self-revelatory work, Sheila has experienced the 'gift', which she identifies with one of Walcott's favourite symbols, the moon: 'I was the moon. I gave out a light that didn't burn but showed everything clearly' (p. 238). Ironically, the experience eventually makes her reject the theatre for a while: in her religious phase she subscribes to an ancient anti-theatrical prejudice, telling her former colleagues that 'To change our voices, that's idolatry; to be someone else for money is harlotry. How can we be another till we find ourselves?' (p. 282). Even more ironically, this last sentence could as well be the demand of the actress bent on perfecting her art as of the religious zealot; for as she later makes clear to Harvey, the moment of vocational revelation when she played Cleopatra was also one of intense self-revelation.

Though all her colleagues recognize the reality of this 'gift' in the actor's life, and its presence in Sheila, they have varying feelings about and estimates of their work in the theatre and of its function and value in Trinidad. Again, the authorial statement is given to Phil, who summons 'brimstone and ashes' on 'a government that don't give a fart ... for its artists, on a people you have to remind to find some pride'; nevertheless: 'if it was in my power to sprinkle benediction on your kind ... you knows I would, and I would do the same for every actor, every entertainer, because they do incorporate man's suffering inside their own; they does drive theirselves to the point of madness to make confusion true' (p. 300). But less idealistically and more immediately there is the problem of what kind of theatre to make in Trinidad. This is presented not as a merely theoretical debate but as a highly personal issue for the characters that produces one of the most dramatically charged confrontations of the play. Chris, the writer of 'West Indian back-yard comedy' – one of which the cast is rehearsing alongside *Antony and Cleopatra* – rejects Shakespeare and the rest of the classic Western repertoire because it has nothing to do with 'the life of all them black people out in the hot sun on Frederick Street at twelve o'clock trying to hustle a living' (p. 246). Gavin, whose sense of integrity as black man and actor has brought him back from his profitable but self-despising career in the States, accuses him of wasting his talent in the process, of losing his seriousness as a writer and becoming a 'clown'. Furious, Chris tells him that his experience in the States has made him a 'schizophrenic nigger', and that at least the kind of drama he writes 'would have restored you to your origins, your roots, your language, your childhood, because ... that's where every artist starts from' (p. 250). But Chris subsequently undergoes a radical change in his own artistic direction: he retires to Barbados and his English wife, but he writes a play about the company (to be understood perhaps as not unlike Walcott's own?), that is closely based on their experience together.

Walcott's play offers a variety of responses to the dilemma of serious post-colonial artists, their situation persistently provoking anxieties of inferiority and 'second-handedness' aroused by their knowledge of metropolitan culture and exacerbated by working in a cultural environment that is their own but that enjoys neither official encouragement nor popular sympathy or approval. If the dominant sentiment likely to be engendered in an audience is the positive assertion of the actor's, and theatre's, 'holy' function, associated with Sheila and the final image of her resuming work on a deserted stage, *A Branch of the Blue Nile* leaves room for – indeed insists on – other possibilities. Marylin, without Sheila's integrity, goes off to the States to become another 'black actress' exploited by the system there; Gavin's move to teaching seems to be a retreat, an at least temporary confession of defeat; and Harvey, the catalyst of all this and the one who once spoke so idealistically about the need for them to purge themselves 'of fear, of cowardice, envy, self-contempt, conceit', returns in disillusionment to a job in England and to a no doubt symbolic early death.

The dilemma of the seriously aspiring artist in the West Indies is also a main preoccupation in *The Last Carnival* (1982), though here the artist is a painter and a member of white French Creole society. Victor and his brother Oswald are scions of an old planter family, living on their beautiful estate in the Santa Rosa valley as well as owning a fine townhouse in Port of Spain. Agatha Willett, a young Englishwoman of working-class origin and socialist opinion, arrives as the governess to Victor's two children, their mother having died of malaria. The action spans the period from 1948, when Agatha arrives and first comes under the spell of this, for her, novel and exotic way of life, through Independence Day in 1962 to Carnival Day in 1970. In the course of it Victor commits suicide, his failure as a painter having driven him insane, and Agatha becomes something of a post-colonial *grande dame*, the friend of a cabinet minister who was once her servant, and a profound but troubled influence on the lives of Victor's now adult children, Clodia and Tony, as well as of Sydney, the servant boy who becomes a leader of the Black Power guerrillas fighting in the hills.

If, as a French Creole, Victor has a different personal and artistic relationship both to Trinidadian and metropolitan culture from black artists like Jordan and Sheila, the result is similar – the sense of an all-pervading provincial mediocrity, the anxiety that nothing, in the art of this place, can be genuinely original and alive. In Victor's case mimicry becomes obsession and finally madness. He tries to paint his own paradise, Santa Rosa, as Watteau 'painted his whole culture, as if it were a sunset'. Showing Agatha a projection of the *Embarkation to Cythera* he asks: 'You see those pilgrims in the painting? They can't move. It's like some paralyzed moment in a carnival' (p. 17). Later, Victor tries to recreate such a moment in the local carnival, dressing up himself, Agatha, Oswald and the servants in period costumes and enacting a short performance around Baudelaire's poem on the same subject. To his brother's objection that 'Carnival is Carnival and art is art' he insists that 'I am only asking for one moment of stillness, one moment of meaning, in all the noise. Two minutes of silence to remind us of our origins' (p. 42). But the idea flops, subverted by the vulgar hilarity of the would-be performers; and Victor is left alone in his Watteau costume, shouting his disgust at an imagined audience of his fellow Creoles, prefiguring his descent into a madness in which he believes himself to be the painter.

There are different estimates made in the play of Victor's talent as an artist and the value of his work in relation to Trinidadian culture. But in his own eyes he is a failure, and he associates his art with death: 'You know, I have come to realize what's wrong with my work', he tells Agatha as they sit watching a cricket match celebrating Independence Day. 'I am not an artist but a mortician. I paint all of this, the pasture, the mango trees getting rusty, the church spire, the cricket field, how many times I've painted them, and everything I touch with my brush is born dead!' (p. 50). If some of this is due to the psychological legacy of his pregnant wife's death and perhaps simply to a lack of sufficient talent, Victor's failure and madness are also the product of his love-hate relationship both with French culture and with Trinidad. He worships his European artistic heritage, loves the natural beauty of his native land, but shares the Creoles' 'hatred of the colonial for the metropole' (p. 10), and at the same time is disgusted by the inadequacies of his people and their culture. Even Independence will alter nothing for Creoles like himself: unlike black Trinidadians, he tells Agatha, 'we can't change.

Never to be independent. We will remain colonials' (p. 50). Many years later Victor's son, himself a designer, offers his verdict on his father and his inheritance: 'He made us cherish taste, and it was the wrong taste for this country, and that makes us useless' (p. 73).

If Victor's cultural isolation and ambivalence take the most extreme form – a theatricalization of the self that extends into madness – he is not the only character who is caught, like the pilgrims in Watteau's painting, in 'some paralyzed moment in a carnival', in a performance that is also a kind of stasis. Agatha Willett (the name suggests both the initial aspiration to 'goodness' and the desire to achieve it) has her conscience suffocated, as she feared (p. 20), by the beauty of Santa Rosa and the role she is able to play in it. The gross but honest Oswald early on identifies the contradiction and perhaps the motive: 'Miss Willett after a sweaty day with the natives climbing into a mahogany four-poster and reading Marx by an antique lamp, glowing after her hot bath in her porcelain tub . . . They need protection from your third-class remorse' (p. 30). Third-class remorse or not, the desire to change things is real enough, as are the results of the school on the verandah and the instruction to the servants to be less deferential. But with time Agatha freezes into a 'character', a necessary role in the post-colonial scenario, even a defender of the reactionary white establishment she once detested, or affected to. 'I hope to God you didn't find me charming', she asks the journalist Brown, who has come to do a piece on Victor's work. The self-consciousness about her position in this society, in her per- formance as the guardian of Victor's memory, is symptomatic of what she becomes after his death.

There are others 'performing' too, playing an image of them- selves in the Trinidadian 'Carnival'. Clodia's role is 'the dissolute heiress', until she decides she doesn't want to end like Agatha and leaves the island. Jean, the servant who becomes a politician and subsequently a cabinet minister, is still, as Agatha proudly proclaims, her creation, socially and, from what we hear, politically. Though Sydney's active commitment to the revolutionary cause seems to set him apart and to suggest his escape from the common syndrome, he is presented as, in fact, Agatha's main victim. On the run, he comes to the house, even though he has rejected everything it stands for and even his old name. Ostensibly, he has come to get a horse to aid his escape, but when his uncle asks if he came to look for Miss Willett he replies: 'Yes, yes, I feel something drew me here to see Miss Agatha' (p. 78), and laments that 'she ain't here to see the Sydney that she wanted'. Clodia confirms it later when she tells Agatha: 'He asked for you. Like he was showing his teacher what he had learnt' (p. 90). Even revolutionary activity, it's suggested, is borrowed clothing; 'another Carnival', according to the young black journalist Brown. The only escape is the boat out, which in the last scene of the play Clodia is waiting to take.

These plays are not without their dramatic weaknesses. *The Last Carnival*, the richest of them, works well in its first half, in the story of Agatha and her encounter with Victor and his household in a new, strange and stirring land. But it is open to the charge, like *Remembrance*, of being too perfunctory and schematic in its action in act two, and the characters of being sometimes too self-consciously wordy. A similar implausibility of plot and character relationship also bedevils *Pantomime* and *A Branch of the Blue Nile*. Nevertheless, taken together, they constitute a sustained and deeply serious exploration of the dilemmas facing artists in the West Indies and through this a portrait of the wider condition of that culture, and the quarrels that its intellectuals cannot avoid having with it. Walcott dramatizes the artist's disenchantment and creative failure – a failure that is always personal as well as artistic. But the failure is balanced, or at least qualified, by the hope embodied in the younger generation. There is a moment in *Pantomime* when Jackson, enraged at Harry's question about how he knows that Crusoe believes in his ultimate redemption, shouts: *'Because, you fucking ass, he has faith!'* (p. 147). If there is Jordan's failure there is also Frederick's insistence that he will stay on the island and paint. If Harvey leaves for England and death, Sheila chooses the theatre and life in Trinidad. If the plays persistently dramatize creative frustration and failure they also go some way towards endorsing Walcott's own faith in the function and power of art, expressed in his remarkable assertion in 'What the Twilight Says' that the 'future of West Indian militancy lies in art' (p. 18).

The quarrel with West Indian reality has not been, for Walcott, the exclusive preoccupation of the artist and intellectual. Exploiting the theatrical possibilities of popular and folk form he has also dramatized the conflict between West Indians who are in no way members of a social or literary elite and the forces of 'progress', represented by the coalition of foreign capital and local businessmen. In the musical *O Babylon!* (1976), on which Walcott collaborated with Galt MacDermot, the composer of *Hair!* the struggle is between a community of Rastas awaiting a visit from their 'living Jah', the Emperor Haile Selassie, and the entrepreneurs who want to build a luxury hotel on their 'Zion'. In *Beef, No Chicken* (1981), which is formally not unlike the sort of 'back-yard comedy' Chris wrote in *A Branch of the Blue Nile*, the symbol of 'progress' is the road being constructed by the Mongroo Construction Company through the sleepy town of Couva in central Trinidad. If the pressure towards modernization – with its capacity for lining the pockets of the local elite – is in each case ultimately triumphant, it is not without a fight. And in both plays the popular struggle is rooted in cultural values that have organically evolved through history. A character in *Beef, No Chicken* puts it succinctly, as he describes a history lesson given to his charges by the eccentric schoolmaster Franco:

> Have them parked on one side of the road. Where the silk
> cotton tree was. He have the whole class looking down in the
> hole, teaching them about the past. Well, history is a deep hole
> ... Last week that big tree gave them shade and strength.
> Today them poor school children standing there in the blazing
> sun with all their roots gone. (p. 120)

But the finest of Walcott's experiments in popular and folk form – and his masterpiece to date – is *Dream on Monkey Mountain* (1967), in which he develops his earlier achievement in portraying the elemental struggles of Trinidadian peasants. In the process he transmutes folk form into a complex, poetic evocation of the psychology of cultural subjugation and the desire for liberation.

Even more so than with most plays, plot summary and selective quotation are inadequate in conveying the theatrical experience of

Dream on Monkey Mountain. In 'A Note on Production' introducing the published text, Walcott implicitly indicates the difficulties involved and at least offers some preliminary guidance on how it should be read or produced: 'The play is a dream, one that exists as much in the given minds of its principal characters as in that of its writer, and as such, it is illogical, derivative, contradictory. Its source is metaphor and it is best treated as a physical poem with all the subconscious and deliberate borrowings of poetry' (p. 208). Like a dream it resists description and interpretation: it can, and should, mean different things to different people, or even different things to the same person at different times.

The prologue introduces us to an old man, Makak, who has been arrested and jailed for smashing up a café. The Corporal and Makak's cellmates, Tigre and Souris, form a mock court of prosecutor and judges, but when Makak comes to make his deposition his cage is flown out of sight and as he tells his vision its subject – 'this woman, / The loveliest thing I see on this earth, / Like the moon walking along her own road' (p. 227) – appears and then withdraws. This is the 'dream' – or is it? – that he has had on Monkey Mountain, which has caused him to go berserk and in his madness claim to be 'the direct descendant of African kings, a healer of leprosy and the Saviour of his race' (p. 225).

As he describes how the overwhelming effect of the apparition makes him fall unconscious to the ground, the scene changes and the action takes over from Makak's narrative. He is woken by Moustique, who has come to collect his business partner to sell their charcoal at market. Makak tells his sceptical, down-to-earth friend of his early morning encounter with the white woman, which he insists was not a dream. She amazed him, he confides, by calling out his name, 'my real name. A name I do not use' (p. 235), and revealing that she knows everything about him. She promised him 'that if I want her, she will come and live with me, and I take her in my arms, and I bring her here' (p. 236). Most important of all for Makak she tells him, as they sit by their fire, that he should no longer live alone in the forest, 'frighten of people because I think I ugly', since he comes from 'the family of lions and kings' (p. 236). When Moustique finds a white mask with long, coarse hair in the hut, Makak, who denies ever having seen it before, comes to a decision: 'Saddle my horse, if you love me, Moustique, and cut a sharp bamboo for me, and put me on that horse, for Makak will ride to the edge of the world, Makak will walk like he used to in Africa, when his name was lion!' (p. 240).

Like a latter-day Don Quixote and Sancho Panza, Makak and Moustique sally forth. On their travels Makak cures an apparently mortally sick man by holding a hot coal in one hand and touching the man's head with the other, telling the villagers that 'You are living coals, / you are trees under pressure, / you are brilliant diamonds / In the hand of your God' (p. 249). He is overwhelmed by the power he now possesses, but Moustique's attitude is entirely mercenary: 'I see a sick man with snake bite, and a set o' damn asses using old-time medicine. I see a road paved with silver' (p. 253). By the time they reach Quatre Chemin market, Makak's exploits are already the stuff of popular legend. But Moustique's greed brings disaster: impersonating Makak he lifts a bowl to his lips only for a spider to run over his hand. He is deeply shaken, for he has already inadvertently picked up a spider and her eggs, an omen of death, in Makak's hut and been warned by Basil, the top-hatted figure of death, that 'We go meet again, stranger.' His imposture discovered, the crowd beats him mercilessly. He dies, Makak letting out *'a terrible cry of emptiness'* as he gazes into his dead friend's eyes. Moustique's body is removed by a band of demons that includes the figure of a woman wearing the mask that has inspired Makak as he writhes on the ground in a fit.

The action of part two returns to the prison cells, Makak lying in his cage moaning and muttering to himself in his sleep. He pleads with the Corporal to release him, offering him money that he has hidden away. Encouraged in his delusion of African kingship by Souris and Tigre, who are after his money, Makak draws a knife and murders Corporal Lestrade – only for the Corporal to return miraculously to life and set off in enthusiastic pursuit of his prey. In the forest, in the primeval darkness, even Tigre and Souris are afraid. And its effect on the Corporal is to make him completely mad, as he imagines himself a white bwana out hunting the natives. In the moonlight he meets the sinister coffin maker, Basil, and is made to confess his sins: 'Too late have I loved thee, Africa of my mind ... I jeered thee because I hated half of myself, my eclipse' (p. 299). He seeks and is offered forgiveness by Makak, only for Tigre to reveal his true motives in coming to the forest. Souris refuses to follow him, saying that 'His madness worth more to me than your friendship. Are you sure where you are, Tigre, are you sure who you are?' (p. 303). But the revelation that Tigre only wanted his money immobilizes Makak, who confesses he is lost and has forgotten the way. He has surrendered his dream of Africa, and admits that he is 'lonely, lost, an old man again', looking forward to morning when 'the dream will rise like vapour, the shadows will be real, you will be corporal again, you will be thieves, and I an old man, drunk and disorderly, beaten down by a Bible, and tired of looking up to heaven' (p. 304). Horrified by his new vision – of his own people 'devouring their own entrails like the hyena, eaten with self-hatred' (p. 305) – Makak is himself now only a 'shadow' driven forward by the Corporal, who has murdered Tigre and become transformed into the black version of his former 'white' self: 'Bastard, hatchet-man, opportunist, executioner', the figure always discreetly placed behind black dictators, orchestrating the 'splendour, barbarism, majesty, noise, slogans, parades' that are used to oppress their own people and drown out the truth.

In a climactic scene of apotheosis, Makak is the unwilling recipient of the extravagant tribute of his people, glorified as the 'inventor of history' itself. The 'accused' are presented, an absurd jumble of names from Plato through to Sir Cecil Rhodes and Tarzan, their common crime being that they were white. Moustique is brought in, accused by the Corporal of having 'betrayed our dream'. But he in turn accuses Makak of betraying his dream: 'Once you loved the moon, now a night will come when, because it white, from your deep hatred you will want it destroyed' (p. 315). He is led away, to be replaced by Makak's apparition, the white woman. He begs to know who she is but receives no response, except the Corporal's insistence that she be beheaded – which is what Makak does, saying 'Now, O God, now I am free' (p. 320). After a blackout we are returned, in the epilogue, to the prison, to the Corporal and his three prisoners. The confused Makak is answering the Corporal's questions, giving his name as Felix Hobain. Released from custody by the sympathetic Corporal, Felix/Makak shakes his head when asked if he wants the mask with which he has been so obsessed. Accompanied by Moustique, who has arrived worried sick about his old, somewhat crazy friend, Makak begins the walk back to his home on Monkey Mountain.

I have summarized the plot at some length partly because the text of *Dream on Monkey Mountain* is unfortunately not readily available, but also to put some detail on the peculiar dreamlike logic of its structure indicated in Walcott's 'Note on Production'. The overall effect on the audience's response that this dream structure invites is to pervasively call into question the nature and significance of what is being presented. At one level Makak's dream is precisely that: the troubled mental figments, blending his habitual obsessions with distorted versions of reality, of a half-crazed and drunken old man during one night spent in a prison cell with two other petty criminals and a police corporal. But the text in performance seems persistently to elicit another, juxtaposed dimension of response where there is no clear and definitive separation of 'dream' from 'reality'. So in the first scene of act two the audience may reasonably suppose that it is watching a 'realistic' non-dreaming scene, as Makak tries to bribe the Corporal to be released and is encouraged by Tigre, alert at the mention of money, to kill his gaoler. But then, suddenly, the action spirals into something completely unexpected, at least if this is the 'real'; for Makak does indeed kill Lestrade and escapes with the other two convicts into the forest – only for Lestrade to 'resurrect', suggest that this is only what blacks 'dream of', and set off in his new role of scourge of the rebellious natives. The status of what we are seeing and hearing suddenly becomes problematic; we are forced to make an imaginative leap into a space where it is no longer crystal-clear what is indeed 'dream' and what 'reality'.

The effect of this on interpretation is to encourage a pervasive sense of ambivalence towards Makak and his experience: if it is at one level the figment of his troubled, sometimes deranged imagination, it is at another a poetic, necessarily mysterious and perplexing evocation of a collective consciousness. His 'journey' to Africa, inspired by the apparition, and his escape into the forest are both imaginary journeys made only in an old man's drunken and disordered mind *and*, at the same time, symbolic, archetypal quests rooted in the ethnic history and collective consciousness of Caribbean peoples. The miracle cure on the sick villager, likewise, is to be perceived and understood in a necessarily dual response that embraces both Moustique's and the Corporal's cynical interpretations *and* Makak's 'truth', that 'is you all self that is your own enemy', that an oppressed people's renewed self-confidence and faith can indeed work 'miracles'.

Centrally, of course, this duality and ambivalence focus on Makak's vision of the white woman. At one level there is the opposition between Makak's certainty that she is real and Moustique's down-to-earth opinion that 'You had a bad dream, or you sleep outside and the dew seize you' (p. 237). At another, 'poetic' level, there is Makak's early, instinctive answer to his question, 'Tell me please, who are you?', that he will pose repeatedly when she is brought before him at the 'tribunal' – that she is his saviour, who has brought him identity and strength after a lifetime of hiding away from others because of his sense of inferiority:

> Sirs, when I hear that voice,
> singing so sweetly,
> I feel my spine straighten,
> My hand grow strong . . .
> I began to dance,
> With the splendour of a Lion (p. 229)

'And, Moustique, she say something I will never forget,' he adds later: 'She say I should not live so any more, here in the forest, frighten of people because I think I ugly. She say that I come from the family of lions and kings' (p. 236). On the other hand there is Lestrade's answer, that she is a *diablesse*, 'the wife of the devil, the white witch' – in more psychological terms the white Other, 'an image of your longing', everything that is desired because believed to be superior and inaccessible:

> She is lime, snow, marble, moonlight, lilies, cloud, foam and
> bleaching cream, the mother of civilization, and the confounder
> of blackness. I too have longed for her. She is the colour of the
> law, religion, paper, art . . . She is the white light that paralysed

your mind, that led you into this confusion. It is you who
created her, so kill her! (p. 319)

Which Makak does, however regretfully, announcing as he does so
that 'now I am free' (p. 320).

In this case we have some indication of Walcott's thinking
since he introduces the published text of the play with a quotation
from Sartre's introduction to Fanon's *The Wretched of the Earth*:

> Thus in certain psychoses the hallucinated person, tired of
> always being insulted by his demon, one fine day starts hearing
> the voice of an angel who pays him compliments; but the jeers
> don't stop for all that; only, from then on, they alternate with
> congratulations. This is a defence, but it is also the end of the
> story. The self is disassociated, and the patient heads for
> madness.

But this is not the end of the story, interpretatively. For in the
imaginative response that the play seems most likely to elicit,
Makak's vision is imbued with a meaning, a value, that is more than
a psychotic symptom. If it is the voice of psychotic disassociation, it
also seems to offer the beginnings of self-retrieval and resistance to
internalized subjugation: the apparition, after all, addresses Makak by
his proper name (which he had all but forgotten), gives him the
confidence to leave the forest and become a sociable being again, and
in general inspires him with a pride in his heritage and historical
identity that can certainly lead to the 'madness' of the apotheosis
scene but which is also the basis of a valid and necessary ethnic self-
esteem. Significantly, it is Lestrade, who in both his 'white' and
'black' incarnations is truly self-hating and psychotic, who demands
that Makak behead the woman. If, as a result, he is 'free', it is a
freedom that is also a terrible loss, as Makak seems to realize.

In the last moments of *Dream on Monkey Mountain*, Makak
asks for personal effacement so that his mythic identity may be
perpetuated and others may say that 'Makak lives where he has
always lived, in the dream of his people' (p. 326). And indeed by the
end of the play Walcott's hero has assumed imaginatively something

of the mythic dimension accorded certain characters in folk-tales and folklore. It is no longer Makak who is the dreamer but the audience, which has had presented in theatrical images its own 'dream' of subjugation and desire for liberation. Formally, it is a remarkable achievement. It combines the drama of consciousness of the modern Western dream play with the conventions of West Indian folk story; the world of Frantz Fanon with the firelit face of the storyteller in the village compound. And in its content it is the richest of all Walcott's dramatic portraits of characters quarrelling with West Indian reality. The richest and the most fundamental, for the quarrel here is with that deepest part of the self in which the dream of self-liberation contends with the demons of internalized subjugation.

August Wilson's theatre of the blues

Visitors to Washington, DC may well be struck by the fact that only a mile or so away from the White House and the Capitol Building, the political centres of power in the world's richest and most powerful state, there are the ghetto slums of a predominantly black city, whose communities often live in conditions more akin to the Third World than the First. The same is true of other American cities, the largely black populations of Harlem or Watts for example, inhabiting in crucial respects a different world, a different reality from those mainly white, middle-class people who live sometimes only a few blocks away in New York and Los Angeles. Periodically, as we know, the frustrations, resentments and anger accompanying these extraordinary material discrepancies within the same society have exploded into large-scale race riots and rebellions. But even when American cities with large black populations are 'peaceful', the simmering discontents hardly breaking the surface of routine life, there are still constant reminders of black deprivation not only in the obvious material appearances of poverty, but in the soaring crime rates, the violence on the streets, the prevalence of such ills as drug and alcohol abuse and prostitution, and the statistics relating to employment, education and health.

While much has been done to come to grips with some of these problems – not least by black communities themselves, through a range of neighbourhood-based organizations – and though there have been localized successes, it cannot be said that the picture as a whole is encouraging or progressively improving. Indeed, many knowledgeable commentators would say that, if anything, the reverse is the case. At the cultural – or perhaps one should say subcultural –

level such an economic and political climate has encouraged the development among black youth of styles of dress and behaviour, of music and dance – rap and 'hip hop', for example – as well as spray-paint art, the pop video and other such popular and 'street' forms that assertively express both an aggressive resistance to what is perceived as a dominant and hostile white society and an equally forceful sense of contemporary black identity.

What we are witnessing now in the great cities of America is only the most recent phase of a continuous historical process that began with slavery. In this, black Americans, in the context of what they largely believe to be a hostile, exploitative white culture, seek to assert their distinctive identity and their right to belong as equals in American society. It is a struggle that has necessarily assumed a variety of dimensions – political, economic and cultural – and which has gone through several historical phases, including in more recent times the great Civil Rights marches and campaigns of the 1950s and sixties led by the Reverend Martin Luther King, and the Black Power movement of the 1960s and seventies. If the Civil Rights Movement was largely Southern-based and 'integrationist', seeking to end discriminatory practices against blacks in the more reactionary states in a largely Christian spirit of equality and fraternity, Black Power and its present-day successors such as the Nation of Islam have been more urban, more militant movements, which have responded to the perceived failure of white-dominated society to permit blacks economic and social equality even in the apparently more demo-cratic, advanced and liberal cities of the North and California. In some of its manifestations the contemporary Black Consciousness movement in America has embraced a philosophy of cultural and even political separatism, firmly rejecting the fundamental aim of Martin Luther King and his associates, which was the establishment of equal rights, as hopelessly inadequate in social terms and even as harmful to the existential and cultural identity of black people.

Unsurprisingly, black artistic culture in America has been profoundly affected by these political and ideological currents within the black struggle. In a society where 'white' artistic and entertain-ment forms have been all-powerful, and able to incorporate (and often travesty) such originally black forms as jazz, the blues and the minstrel show, there has been a persistent struggle to achieve authentic black self-expression, in distinctively black artistic forms, alongside enforced co-option. In the theatre this has involved – even as black artists have sought recognition in and by mainstream American theatre – a long struggle to establish an exclusively black dramatic repertory performed by professional black companies for black, or at least predominantly black, audiences. It has also, especially in recent years, produced a desire for, and identification of, an allegedly distinct black dramatic and theatrical aesthetic.

The 1960s was the crucial decade for black American theatre in both respects. In the effort to establish itself, black theatre underwent a radical departure from the 'liberal' model, based on the white mainstream, to another, politically more militant and separatist one, which sought to establish black theatres in the midst of black communities, where they could perform work that would educate and raise the consciousness of an oppressed people to form a black 'nation'. The issue of a distinctively black aesthetic was directly related to this new 'model' and its inspiration in the political ideology of Black Consciousness. The emphasis now, at least in its more radical version, was not so much on the need for black equality with whites as on black *difference*, the uniqueness of black culture, of black identity. To give artistic expression to this liberated identity required, some believed, a complete break with a white-dominated theatre aesthetic, and a return to African roots.

One play, with its accompanying manifesto 'The Revolutionary Theatre', crystallized all of these innovations: LeRoi Jones's (Amiri Baraka's) *Dutchman*, which opened off-Broadway in 1964. In his typically overheated rhetoric, Jones's manifesto exhorted practitioners of the 'Revolutionary Theatre' (the author is much given to both capital letters and exclamation marks) to 'Accuse and Attack anything that can be accused and attacked' – especially if, as it usually is, it is white. *Dutchman*, and Baraka's other plays of the period such as *The Slave* and *Black Mass*, fulfil his own prescription, as does the contemporary work of other black dramatists, notably Ed Bullins, committed to the creation of a 'revolutionary' theatre. In *Dutchman* Lula, the antagonist of Baraka's black protagonist Clay, is a white bitch who enjoys playing with and taunting a black who can never win. At the play's climax, Clay, who recognizes that blacks have been forced neurotically to bottle up their anger or deflect it into such forms as jazz or the blues, is driven into a rage by Lula's provocations. But his self-liberation, his awareness of his murderous black consciousness, comes too late: before he can kill her, Lula stabs him, white America destroying what could be a real threat to itself.

If a play such as *Dutchman* departs radically in content and viewpoint from the drama of black writers such as Langston Hughes or Lorraine Hansberry, which had hitherto enjoyed some critical and commercial success, it also represents something new at formal and stylistic levels. Ed Bullins, interviewed in the late 1960s, believed that 'our art will be completely different from White Anglo-Saxon Western art' in no more than a decade.[1] Unlike in music, where difference was established from the beginning, black theatre had inevitably been moulded by inherited white Euro-American traditions. The familiar elements of the 'well-made' drama – linear plot reaching a well-defined climax, characterization based on detailed portrayal of the individual personality, allegory and symbolism, if present at all, subdued to the demands of realism, the absence of music, dance and spectacle – were to be disparaged and eschewed. In their place Baraka and others advocated what they believed was a distinctively black aesthetic, ultimately inherited from African art, with what they took to be its ritualistic and functional characteristics. Black music in particular was a profound source of inspiration and an aesthetic model. For the theorists of the 'Revolutionary Theatre', the theatre, indeed the art, of black Americans should be like the blues, or traditional African sculptures, which convey the essence of the community's spirit, its ethos, in a direct, emotive but highly functional manner.

It is somewhat ironic, then, that America's leading contemporary black dramatist, August Wilson, seems to owe little or nothing, formally, to this championing of a black aesthetic. Wilson's plays, at least thus far, are almost classically 'well-made', with

---

[1] Marvin X, 'Interview with Ed Bullins', *New Plays from the Black Theatre*, New York: Bantam Books, 1969, p. xii.

strongly individualized characters and realistic settings and action. This is perhaps especially surprising given that Wilson was initially drawn to the theatre because of its power as a platform for expressing his Black Power political views in the late 1960s and early seventies; and because he has continued to emphasize both the African roots of black American identity, and to be inspired by jazz and the blues. If Wilson's work is to be seen as militant, it is in a quite different way from, say, Baraka's. Spanning most of the first half of this century, his plays depict the experiences of black Americans who have migrated from the South to the urban centres of the Northern USA. All of them – *Ma Rainey's Black Bottom*, *Fences*, *Joe Turner's Come and Gone* and *The Piano Lesson* – present characters who are forced to confront the consequences of a double historical trauma: the brutalities of the Southern heritage and the injustice and inequalities of the North as they struggle to make a home for themselves, to achieve an identity, and to lead free and dignified lives in their new environment.

The harsh economic and social realities of life for blacks who have moved north constitute a persistent dramatic presence in Wilson's plays. In *Ma Rainey's Black Bottom* (1984) the black struggle for economic equality and cultural self-expression is centred on the music business in Chicago in the late 1920s, and specifically on a recording session involving the black blues singer Ma Rainey, her band, her white manager Irvin, and the owner of the recording company, Sturdyvant. Throughout, there is a battle going on between the races for control both of the nature of the music and its commercial exploitation. Sturdyvant's attitude is clear from his opening conversation with Ma Rainey's manager:

STURDYVANT: She's your responsibility. I'm not putting up with any Royal Highness ... Queen of the Blues bullshit!
IRVIN: Mother of the Blues, Mel. Mother of the Blues.
STURDYVANT: I don't care what she calls herself. I'm not putting up with it. I just want to get her in here ... record those songs on that list ... and get her out. Just like clockwork, huh? (p. 132)

For him music is merely a business ('two more years and I'm gonna get out ... get into something respectable. Textiles'), and the black artists are merely erratic and troublesome means, requiring rigorous control, to a profitable end. Irvin is more subtle and, apparently, sensitive in his approach to Ma Rainey and the musicians, but again only as a means to a mercenary end. As she points out, in the six years he has been her manager he has only once invited her to his house, and that was to sing for his friends. If she behaves imperiously, brooking no compromise, it is because she has no illusions about the real nature of her relationship with the white-owned and white-controlled record industry:

> They don't care nothing about me. All they want is my voice. Well, I done learned that, and they gonna treat me like I want to be treated no matter how much it hurt them. They back there now calling me all kinds of names . . . calling me everything but a child of god. But they can't do nothing else. They ain't got what they wanted yet. As soon as they get my voice down on them recording machines, then it's just like if I'd be some whore and they roll over and put their pants on. Ain't got no use for me then. (p. 191)

Ma's confrontational and ruthless attitude to the whites even extends to her own people, if they show signs of threatening her interests. She sacks the ambitious young trumpeter Levee for his insubordination in wishing to change the arrangement of her song 'Ma Rainey's Black Bottom', and in general to adapt what he regards as their old-fashioned, tent-show, jug-band music to the changing tastes of the more sophisticated North. Levee has taken to his new environment with apparently self-confident relish. He wants to form his own band playing his own style of music, and to get it he is prepared, unlike Ma Rainey, to make compromises with white business and musical tastes. But he fails to learn the lesson that determines Ma Rainey's behaviour – that people like Sturdyvant will use blacks and drop them as they find convenient. He makes the mistake of reposing too much trust in Sturdyvant who has asked him to write some songs and promised to let him record them, only to go back on his undertaking.

The conflict between Ma Rainey and her young trumpeter is not just one of personal interest but, more generally, of differing attitudes towards whites and life in the North. And this larger clash of values emerges in specific relation to the music they play, and in particular to its ownership. Levee wants to exercise his personal creativity, but he also wants to cater to popular Northern taste. His music, as Irvin explains to Ma, 'gives the people what they want. It gets them excited . . . makes them forget about their troubles' (p. 176). Music, and its creative artistry, are viewed by Levee primarily as entertainment, feeding the desire for escapism and excitement – just as they are in business terms, by Irvin and Sturdyvant. And he therefore, quite logically, concedes the artist's subordination to the businessman ('Hell, the man's the one putting out the record! He's gonna put out what he wanna put out!' (p. 151)). But for Ma Rainey, who is indifferent to changing Northern tastes, music is a distinctive way of living and even of mastering life:

> White folks don't understand about the blues. They hear it
> come out, but they don't know how it got there. They don't
> understand that's life's way of talking. You don't sing to feel
> better. You sing 'cause that's a way of understanding life . . .
> This be an empty world without the blues. I take that
> emptiness and try to fill it up with something. (pp. 194–5)

No one, therefore, can 'own' this music – certainly not Sturdyvant, who as a white understands nothing about it and only wishes to make money out of it; and not even Ma herself, even though she's known as the Mother of the Blues: 'I ain't started the blues way of singing. The blues always been here' (p. 195).

In Wilson's other plays, too, the black characters contend daily for basic control of their new lives in the North. It is a struggle, as Berniece puts it in *The Piano Lesson*, for people who are 'at the bottom of life'. Troy Maxson, in *Fences*, fights his employers – and wins – to gain promotion from garbage collector to driver of the garbage truck. Seth, in *Joe Turner's Come and Gone*, aspires to own a small business making pots and pans, but is refused a loan except on extortionate terms. On the other hand Avery, the ambitious young preacher in *The Piano Lesson*, gets his loan to establish his new church. Wilson presents varying outcomes to his characters' struggles to rise from the bottom of a white-dominated society, just as he endows them with differing values, attitudes and aspirations. But their common condition is one of struggle against the racism, corruption and predatory materialism of white America. Ma Rainey may be exceptional in having achieved economic independence and control of her own destiny; but she is no more immune from the racism of a white cab-driver or the corruption of a white policeman than is Jeremy, the penniless young black worker of *Joe Turner*.

But the hardships and injustices of his characters' lives in the North are only one dimension of Wilson's dramatic treatment of black American experience in the first half of this century. Another, which is always crucially important in his plays, is their memories of the sufferings they endured, personally and as a race, before their migration, and the ways in which these have affected their lives in the present.

Levee's readiness to 'sell his soul to the devil' (p. 157) by compromising with white society to achieve his ambitions, his subsequent disappointment and its fatal aftermath, are the product of a particular temperament but also of a particular history – his family's brutal experience of oppression in the South. His long speech about the traumatic event of his childhood, and the moral he has drawn from it, forms the climax of the first half of the play. He describes how, while his father was away, his mother was gang-raped by whites who considered his father 'an uppity nigger'; how he tried to intervene and was scarred across the chest by a knife; and how his father took his revenge on at least some of the assailants before being caught, lynched and burned:

> My daddy wasn't spooked up by the white man. Nosir! And
> that taught me how to handle them. I seen my daddy go up and
> grin in this cracker's face ... smile in his face and sell him his
> land. All the while he's planning how he's gonna get him and
> what he's gonna do to him. That taught me how to handle
> them. ... I can smile and say yessir to whoever I please. I got
> time coming to me. (p. 184)

But Levee's wounds are psychological as well as physical, and despite his apparent self-assurance they have never fully healed. His reaction to the story about the Reverend Gates's humiliation by whites is to pour out his hatred of a God who seems to protect whites, and to provoke a fight with the normally placid Cutler, threatening him with a knife.

Levee's deeply felt personal quarrel with what he believes is a white man's God brings on tragedy after his rebuff by a white man he thought he knew how to handle. The immediate catalyst is trivial and absurd; one of his colleagues steps on his new shoes, of which he is inordinately proud. The anger and frustration he feels at the dashing of his hopes by Sturdyvant – behind which lies the whole history of white brutality to his family – explodes into violence. In a rage he rushes at Toledo and plunges the knife into his back. Levee and Toledo are in their different ways the victims of a cycle of violence initiated by whites in the South but perpetuated, now by black on black, in the North.

It is particularly ironic that Levee kills the play's philosopher and *raisonneur* of the black condition. Alone of the characters, Toledo has educated himself into an articulate, coherent under-standing of his people's history and contemporary situation. As a result he is able, truthfully, to tell Levee: 'I know what you talking about, but you don't know what I'm talking about' (p. 138); and to reproach Slow Drag with 'There's so much that goes on around you and you can't even see it' (p. 146). Toledo has difficulty penetrating the ignorance of all his colleagues but especially that of Levee, who persistently fails to understand or else rejects his analysis of black American history and its implications. His message – and evidently the dramatist's – is that not only Levee but all of them have been 'spooked up' by the white man, and in the process have lost their authentic identity. Though Slow Drag might unconsciously retain African ways of conceptualizing – 'an ancestral retention' – he has forgotten 'the name of the gods': 'We done sold Africa for the price of tomatoes. We done sold ourselves to the white man in order to be like him. ... We done sold who we are in order to become someone else. We's imitation white men' (p. 206). They are nothing, he says, but 'the leftovers', the unwanted remains of the white man's feast. The problem, as he sees it, isn't with the whites but with blacks who 'don't know that we been took and made history out of' (p. 172). If the crucial question now is: 'What's the colored man gonna do with himself?', the prerequisite for any meaningful action to resolve this

49

question is collective self-knowledge: 'first we gotta know we the leftovers' (p. 171). Only then might it be possible for blacks to reassess their own attitudes and behaviour, particularly their – for Toledo – 'sickening' preoccupation with 'having a good time', and take purposeful collective action.

It is, in a way, appropriate then that Levee's violence is aimed at Toledo, since they represent antagonistic values and aspirations. The one preaches the need for a distinctive identity that is not an imitation of whiteness, based on a sense of black history and the African heritage; the other seeks incorporation into white society. The incident with the shoes, which sparks off Levee's violence, is absurdly trivial but also symbolic, indicating the gulf separating their two attitudes. Earlier in the play, when they discuss his sharp new shoes, Levee mocks Toledo:

LEVEE: Nigger got them clodhoppers! Old brogans! He ain't nothing but a sharecropper.
TOLEDO: You can make all the fun you want. It don't mean nothing. I'm satisfied with them and that's what counts. (p. 154)

Toledo's shoes, which soil his own and thus bring about the play's violent climax, represent everything Levee wishes and seeks to escape from.

Levee's experience of white oppression in the South is not exceptional, even if its effect on him is. Slow Drag's response to Levee's long speech describing his mother's rape and father's revenge is the musical expression of a collective suffering, which every black character in the play knows:

> If I had my way
> If I had my way
> If I had my way
> I would tear this old building down. (p. 184)

It is the common memory, the historical heritage, informing in one way or another the lives of virtually all the black characters in Wilson's plays. Its most egregious victim, the character who has suffered oppression in its most extreme form, is Herald Loomis of *Joe Turner's Come and Gone* (1986), who has been abducted and forced to serve seven years in Joe Turner's chain gang. As a result he suffers the most intense alienation, which he hopes to end by finding his wife Martha, for whom he has spent four years searching: 'That's the only thing I know to do. I just wanna see her face so I can get me a starting place in the world. The world got to start somewhere. That's what I been looking for. I been wandering a long time in somebody else's world. When I find my wife that be the making of my own' (p. 72).

In a remarkable scene Wilson evokes the effect on his personality of Loomis's years of enslavement. He loses all rational control, inveighs against God but at the same time *'begins to speak in tongues'* and, as he starts to leave, *'is thrown back and collapses, terror-stricken by his vision'* (p. 53). Guided by Bynum Walker, the 'rootworker', Loomis describes what he has seen: bones that rise out of the water and walk on its surface before being washed ashore by a big wave and transformed into black people. It is the vision of one oppressed, deeply troubled individual; but it also has a profoundly representative quality, evoking the collective trauma of which his time in Joe Turner's slave gang is merely a belated historical example – the shipping of Africans across the Atlantic and their enslavement in an alien land. In the vision Loomis sees his body lying with the others and the wind beginning to blow breath into it. He desperately wants to stand up, like the other bodies, and begin his journey along the road, but with increasing desperation he realizes his legs can't carry him, and the first half of the play ends with Loomis collapsing on the floor as the lights go down.

It is a moment signifying the disastrous psychological and spiritual effects that the experience of intense oppression can have on the personality. Loomis at first vehemently denies it when Bynum identifies him as 'one of Joe Turner's niggers': 'You lie! How you see that? I got a mark on me? Joe Turner done marked me to where you can see it?' (p. 71). But Bynum, retaining what the play seems to endorse as the traditional spiritual wisdom of black Americans' African descendants (Loomis recognizes Bynum as 'one of them bones people'), has made a correct identification, seeing in Loomis a man who has 'forgot how to sing your song' (p. 71). And when Loomis asks what made Joe Turner enslave him, Bynum offers an alternative response to Seth's commonsense explanation of slavery, that '[he] just want you to do his work for him. That's all': 'What he wanted was your song. He wanted to have that song to be his. He thought by catching you he could learn that song. Every nigger he catch he's looking for the one he can learn that song from' (p. 73). Enslavement in Bynum's view is other than, or at least more than, a simply economic oppression: it is the coercive expropriation of the black spiritual essence by whites. And the effect of his captivity has been to deprive Loomis of his 'song': 'Now he's got you bound up to where you can't sing your own song. Couldn't sing it them seven years 'cause you was afraid he would snatch it from under you. But you still got it. You just forgot how to sing it' (p. 73).

We will examine in more detail later the importance of Bynum's, and Wilson's, notion of the 'song' and the process by which Herald Loomis recovers his and is able, at last, to stand on his own legs. For the moment it is Bynum's striking interpretation of the history of slavery that is worth dwelling on, since it seems, taking the play as a whole, to have Wilson's authorial endorsement. It is not that Wilson underestimates the economic dimension of white America's historical subjugation of black people – it pervades all his plays, including *Joe Turner*. But through the character of Bynum Walker he invites his audiences to consider the possibility that the oppression of Afro-Americans has had a primarily existential aspect, the product of the whites' predatory desire to 'steal' the blacks' distinctive spiritual and cultural personality, to take from them and exploit for themselves their very essence and identity as people. And if the white man's oppression of blacks has failed to achieve this end, it has at least succeeded, in circumstances such as Loomis's, in subduing that personality and its free expression.

The heritage of oppression in the South is also explored, in tragi-comic form, in *The Piano Lesson* (1988). At the centre of its action stands the upright piano on the legs of which Willie Boy once carved, in the manner of African sculpture, the history of his enslaved family. Owned by the Sutters, who also owned the carver and his family, the piano was 'liberated' by Boy Charles and his brothers on the grounds that 'it was the story of our whole family and as long as

Sutter had it ... he had us' (p. 45). With the arrival at the Northern home of his sister Berniece of both Boy Willie, Boy Charles's son, and the ghost of the latest Sutter mysteriously found dead at the bottom of his well, the piano becomes the object of several struggles: for ownership between white and black, of conflicting views of black Southern history, and about how black people should make use of that historical inheritance in the present and future. For all its humour *The Piano Lesson* is no less pervaded by the sense of a history of violence and suffering and their effects than Wilson's other plays. Apart from the physical brutality there is the emotional oppression of slavery in the form of the enforced separation of enslaved families, like Boy Willie's, on the whim of their owners. In the next generation there is the horror of the whites' revenge on Boy Charles and the others burned in the boxcar, and the apparent retaliation against the white culprits by the so-called 'Ghosts of the Yellow Dog'. And in the present generation there is for Berniece, who has already lost her father to a violent death, the tragedy of her husband Crawley's senseless killing, which she blames on her brother and which accounts for much of the strain in their relationship. Her attitude to this history and therefore to the piano is ambivalent. On the one hand she is horrified and disgusted by the senselessness of the violence that has so scarred her own life: 'All this thieving and killing and thieving and killing. And what it ever lead to? More killing and more thieving. I ain't never seen it come to nothing. People getting burned up. People getting shot. People falling down their wells. It don't never stop' (p. 52). But at the same time she refuses to consider selling the piano – even though at one point she asks why people have died for 'a piece of wood' – on the grounds that '[m]oney can't buy what that piano cost. You can't sell your soul for money' (p. 50).

Her brother's attitude, on the other hand, is that the piano is merely the means to what for him is the most important end – economic independence in the form of the ownership of land that he can farm, in this case land on which his family was once enslaved. Boy Willie is no less firm in his conviction than Berniece, and for reasons which are likewise the product of his and his family's history of oppression:

The world ain't wanted no part of me. . . . The world say it's
better off without me. See, Berniece accept that. She trying to
come up to where she can prove something to the world. Hell,
the world a better place cause of me. . . . So what I got to do? I
got to mark my passing on the road. Just like you write on a
tree, 'Boy Willie was here'. That's all I'm trying to do with that
piano. (pp. 93-4)

Unlike most of Wilson's characters, Boy Willie's residence in
the North is only temporary; he has no desire to stay, and will leave
as soon as he acquires the money to buy Sutter's land. For him the
sale of the piano, and the acquisition of the property are the most
appropriate and effective use of their inheritance, and he is critical of
his sister's attitude towards the piano, which – however emotionally
valid it may be – fails to make any practical use of its economic
potential:

You can't do nothing with that piano sitting up here in the
house . . . Alright now, if you say to me, Boy Willie, I'm using
that piano. I give out lessons on it and that help me make my
rent or whatever. Then that be something else. I'd have to go on
and say, well, Berniece using that piano. She building on it. Let
her go on and use it. (p. 51)

But as he correctly points out, she has never played it the whole time
it has been in the house. Berniece herself explains to Avery why this
is so: when she played it for her mother, she says, 'I used to think
them pictures came alive and walked through the house. Sometime
late at night I could hear my mama talking to them. I said that wasn't
gonna happen to me. I don't play that piano 'cause I don't want to
wake them spirits' (p. 70). Instead, she encourages her daughter
Maretha to play it since she 'don't know nothing about it'. But,
significantly, Maretha can only play by sight and hasn't learnt any
black music (p. 21). In the process of trying to give her daughter a
good start in life Berniece is arguably making her into an 'imitation
white': to make the point, Wilson has Berniece straighten her
daughter's hair with a hot comb during the argument with Boy Willie

about their inheritance and what sort of values should be encouraged in Maretha. For Boy Willie, who has already demonstrated the boogie-woogie to his niece, it is essential that she be told about why and how the carvings were made on the piano so that 'she know where she at in the world' and is proud of her people and colour.

In the end Berniece does play the piano, and with precisely the effect that for so long inhibited her from playing – the waking of the ancestral spirits. She does so to intervene in the climactic struggle between Boy Willie and his other antagonist, the invisible ghost of the white man, Sutter. Throughout the play characters see or are aware of the presence of the ghost, which is evidently haunting the house because of Sutter's belief, in death, that he is the rightful owner of the piano. As Doaker tells Wining Boy, 'Sutter here 'cause of that piano. I heard him playing on it one time. I thought it was Berniece but then she don't play that kind of music' (p. 57). Resisting Boy Willie's attempt to move the piano so as to sell it and buy his land, the ghost engages his opponent in what Wilson's stage direction describes as '*a life-and-death struggle*', throwing him down the stairs and trying to choke him. If Joe Turner, according to Bynum, wanted Herald Loomis's 'song' for his own, Sutter's ghost wants both the piano and its music and, by extension, to prevent his family's former slaves owning his land. And if the effect of his captivity has been to make Loomis unable to sing his own song, Berniece too has renounced playing the piano – and, if Boy Willie is right, some of her own and her daughter's authentic cultural personality. It is only at the very end of the play that she is able, like Loomis, to recover her 'song', and in the process defeat both the ghost and her brother. Sutter's ghost is laid to rest, Boy Willie gives up his attempt to sell the piano, and the instrument in question remains in Berniece's house – though in future, it is hinted, as a *practical* symbol, actively perpetuating the spirit of the people whose images and history are inscribed upon it.

Wilson's characters' memories of suffering and hardship in the South are not, however, exclusively at the hands of whites. The cycle of violence and suffering that Berniece speaks of so feelingly in *The Piano Lesson* may be generated and perpetuated within the black community, and even – perhaps most commonly – within the same family. This is the case with Troy Maxson and his family in *Fences* (1987). Troy tells his friend Bono and his son Lyons of how his father combined a sense of responsibility towards his family with being 'just as evil as he could be' (p. 69). He describes how his father discovered him enjoying the favours of a young woman down by the creek: 'Now I thought he was mad 'cause I ain't done my work. But I see where he was chasing me off so he could have the gal for himself' (p. 70). They fight and his father beats him unconscious:

> When I woke up, I was laying right there by the creek, and
> Blue ... this old dog we had ... was licking my face ... The
> only thing I know was the time had come for me to leave my
> daddy's house. And right there the world suddenly got big.
> And it was a long time before I could cut it down to where I
> could handle it. (pp. 70–1)

In fact Troy has never really learned to handle his world. It is true he has become a sober, hardworking citizen after the experience of poverty in his early days in the city drove him first to theft and then to violent crime, for which he spent fifteen years in prison. But history repeats itself in Troy's relations with his youngest son, Cory. Like his own father he discharges his paternal responsibilities conscientiously but lovelessly, and with a severity that gives some substance to Cory's accusation that 'All you ever did was try and make me scared of you' (p. 104). The culmination of their growing antagonism is trivial but explosive: it comes when Cory's attempt to pass his father on the steps without saying 'excuse me' leads to a physical showdown as they struggle fiercely over a baseball bat. For a moment, it looks as if Troy will repeat his father's beating of him many years before; only at the last moment does he stop himself as he stands over his vanquished son, ready to swing the bat. But it is the end of their relationship, and Cory leaves his home – to return only for his father's funeral – as Troy once left his.

Troy Maxson has an ingrained conviction that his son's aspirations as a sportsman, like his own, are bound to be frustrated by white society: 'I told that boy about that football stuff. The white man ain't gonna let him get nowhere with that football' (p. 26). But he himself frustrates Cory's ambitions, refusing to let him be recruited into college football, and generally failing to understand what his wife Rose persistently tells him: 'Times have changed from when you was young, Troy. People change. The world's changing around you and you can't even see it' (p. 53). *Fences*, the second of his plays but the most recent in historical setting, evokes Wilson's sense that in the fifties and sixties conditions for black Americans were altering significantly, even if they still had to rise from the bottom of society. The tragedy of *Fences* is not so much that of a whole race as of a particular kind of black man, whose personality and conditioning prevent him adapting to change. Thwarted in his own aspirations, frustrated in the fulfilment of some of his strongest desires and needs, Troy estranges his son, his wife and himself. *Fences* is thus tragic in form, as was its predecessor, *Ma Rainey's Black Bottom*, where it is Levee's aspirations in a white-dominated society and his inability to cope with a setback to them that trigger the tragic climax.

But in the two more recent plays tragedy is transcended, even though the protagonists confront a legacy of violence and brutal oppression that is just as intense, if not more so, as in *Ma Rainey* and *Fences*. The ability of Herald Loomis and Berniece to overcome their suffering and achieve some kind of personal liberation or self-realization has to do with the power of music and song, and the special function they have in Wilson's theatre in summoning mysterious powers of recovery and reintegration.

Music is important in all Wilson's plays. As we have seen, *Ma Rainey's Black Bottom* is not only set in the music industry, it is also about what Ma Rainey sings – the blues – and the special significance it has for blacks as 'life's way of talking', 'a way of understanding life' (p. 194). When, at the very end, we hear the sound of Levee's trumpet, now 'muted' but '*struggling for the highest of possibilities and blowing pain and warning*' (Wilson's stage direction, p. 223), the warning is arguably about the hazards of departing, as Levee has done, from the true meaning and function of the blues as the expression of the black American spirit. In *Fences*, music figures prominently in the forms of Troy's song about Blue, which is sung by Cory and Raynell at a decisive moment of self-understanding for the former near the end of the play; in Lyons's devotion to his music, 'cause that's the only way I can find to live in the world' (p. 36); and in

the theatrically climactic moment when the brain-damaged Gabe
blows his trumpet, which has no mouthpiece, to open the gates of
heaven for his dead brother. When no sound emerges Gabe is *'exposed
to a frightful realization'*; Wilson's stage directions continue:

> *He begins to dance. A slow, strange dance, eerie and life-giving.
> A dance of atavistic signature and ritual.* LYONS *attempts to
> embrace him.* GABRIEL *pushes* LYONS *away. He begins to
> howl in what is an attempt at song, or perhaps a song turning
> back into itself in an attempt at speech. He finishes his dance
> and the gates of heaven stand open as wide as God's closet.*
> (p. 119)

However eccentrically worded or (more significantly) problematic
this moment may prove to be in performance, Wilson's text indicates
clearly enough its import and intended effect. Whatever the failures
and disappointments of Troy's life, Gabe is a 'holy fool' capable of
evoking, through his contact in ritualistic dance and song with an
atavistic dimension of being, a redemptive spiritual energy that
transcends the personal tragedy of Troy's life. Like the blues, Gabe's
'music' is what Wilson, in his preface to *Ma Rainey*, describes as 'a
way of being, separate and distinct from any other', something that
'breathes and touches. That connects' (p. 130).

In *Joe Turner* and *The Piano Lesson* the power of this music,
which is also a way of being, and which can be mysteriously elicited
from the ancestral past at crucial moments by certain specially
empowered characters, is enough to bring connection and the
restoration of the integrated self even where there has been a long
history of oppression and alienation. In *Joe Turner* it is Bynum who
possesses this power, through his acquisition of the 'Binding Song'
from his visionary experience on the road with the 'shiny man' and
his father. It is primarily a power, as its name implies, of connection,
or rather reconnection: 'I choose that song because that's what I seen
most when I was travelling . . . people walking away and leaving one
another. So I takes the power of my song and binds them together'
(p. 10). The song, Bynum tells Loomis, was a burden, and initially he
tried to give it back to his father: 'But I found out it wasn't his song. It
was my song. It had come from way deep inside me. I looked long

back in memory and gathered up pieces and snatches of things to make that song. I was making it up out of myself' (p. 71). If his song has been created from the deepest recesses of his self, it is also associated with his powers as a 'rootworker' and the ancestral wisdom and knowledge from which this 'old mumbo jumbo nonsense' (as Seth calls it) originates. Through it he is able to 'bind' Loomis's daughter to her mother Martha and thus bring Loomis and his wife face to face after years of separation, allowing him to 'say my goodbye and make my own world' (p. 90). However, Loomis at first fails to understand what Bynum has done: he believes that Bynum, like Joe Turner and others, has used his song to bind him in the sense of coercing or imprisoning him, and he angrily reacts to this perception by drawing a knife. Bynum explains what is happening: 'You binding yourself. You bound onto your song. All you got to do is stand up and sing it, Herald Loomis. It's right there kicking at your throat. All you got to do is sing it. Then you be free' (p. 91). But it is only after the catharsis of slashing himself across the chest that Loomis realizes he has attained his freedom, or as Wilson's commentating stage direction puts it, has '*accepted the responsibility for his own presence in the world*' (p. 94).

In the climactic moments of *The Piano Lesson*, Berniece is also able to summon up her 'song' to exorcize the ghost of the last member of the white family that for generations oppressed her own, and to resolve the dilemma of how in future to use the piano as the symbol of the black inheritance. Earlier, she has explained to Avery that she has never played the piano since her mother's death because 'I don't want to wake them spirits' (p. 70). But that is precisely what she now does, as she summons the ancestral spirits with the repeated phrase 'I want you to help me' (p. 107). Like Bynum's 'song', it comes from deep within the self and out of history – '*A rustle of wind blowing across the continents*', as Wilson's stage direction has it (p. 106). Her song and music are the means for summoning the power of the ancestral spirits whose histories are carved on the piano, and it is a power that, like that of Bynum's song, makes the singer free. Sutter's ghost is expelled from the house, but we are also to understand that Berniece and her family have achieved a new understanding and cultural empowerment.

August Wilson's drama depicts black Americans struggling – sometimes successfully and sometimes not – to escape from their psychological or spiritual confinement in what Herald Loomis calls 'somebody else's world', and to make it their own. His plays evoke both the conditions that they struggle against and, in moments of intensely theatrical action that embrace the mythic and ritualistic – and which are always associated with the power of music and song – the forces by which cultural emancipation and empowerment may be achieved. The music, and the energies that it arouses, return the characters – and the empathizing audience – to black American roots in Africa and the Southern plantations. In doing so, Wilson challenges black Americans to discover, or perhaps more accurately rediscover, a dimension of being that their subordinated history in a white-dominated society has obscured. These energies are neither easy to define nor to confront: they have to be drawn, piece by piece, from deep within the self, in a hard and potentially tragic quest for personal and racial identity. Their emergence, so all the plays suggest, involves antagonism with what has been a spiritual mainstay of black American culture, the Christian faith. Levee's personal argument with what he believes is a white man's God continues in the later plays. In *Joe Turner's Come and Gone* the religious conflict between the devout Martha and the former deacon Loomis forms the substance of the play's final climax, Loomis inveighing against that '[g]reat big old white man . . . your Mr. Jesus Christ' (p. 92), and responding to Martha's insistence that 'you got to be washed with the blood of the Lamb' by slashing himself and rubbing the blood over his face. And in *The Piano Lesson* Berniece is able to do what the Christian clergyman Avery can't – to intervene decisively to exorcize the ghost of the oppressive white. She draws out of herself, at this moment of crisis, a power that she herself had feared and for so long renounced. It is her 'music', and the 'music' of her forebears; and it is the expression of age-old forces that, Wilson's drama suggests, black Americans must rediscover to achieve their full emancipation from racial subordination.

Jack Davis and the drama
of Aboriginal history

As an invader/settler society, white Australia's artistic culture has
been deeply influenced by its particular experience of colonization.
Where the theatre is concerned, this has meant the domination of its
mainstream and 'art' theatres by foreign products and models (mainly
British) until well into this century. It was only in the late 1960s and
seventies that distinctively Australian voices began to sound in its
theatres, at first in the more experimental 'fringe' venues, interro-
gating, satirically commentating on, but at the same time asserting a
specifically Australian national identity. While hit musicals and
'serious' plays that have had critical and usually commercial success
in the West End or on Broadway continue to appeal to Australian
audiences, the last three decades have witnessed the flourishing of a
genuinely indigenous dramatic culture (in film as much if not more
than in the theatre) that has increasingly reflected and explored the
growing multiculturalism of Australia itself.

One of the main preoccupations of all this dramatic activity
has been the recuperation and reappraisal of Australian history.
Katharine Brisbane, in the introduction to her anthology of recent
Australian drama, justly observes that '[t]he past in the present, the
past bearing down upon the present, is probably the most consistent
theme in contemporary Australian drama'.[1] While such a large and
central theme inevitably has numerous facets, at the centre of
Australian historical consciousness lie the twin traumas accompanying the birth of what was to be the nation: Australia's original

---

[1] Katharine Brisbane, ed., *Australia Plays: New Australian Drama*,
London: Nick Hern Books, 1989, p. xv.

function as a penal colony for Britain, and the devastating impact of white invasion and settlement on the native Aborigines. Both, with varying degrees of intensity, bespeak a history marked by exile, dispossession and a brutal indifference to suffering. Of the two, Australian literary and dramatic culture has explored the former extensively, from almost every conceivable angle, while the latter has been largely ignored and even suppressed.

That the remembrance of things past must embrace, for Australians, the recognition of sustained brutality, oppression and at its worst genocidal horror is at least a thread running through some of – though by no means all – its serious postwar drama. It can be found, for example, even in such a basically genial and popular musical play as Dorothy Hewett's *The Man from Mukinupin* (1979), where the nocturnal killing of Aborigines by the townspeople is testament to the dark side of a culture that in its everyday life is cheerfully, eccentrically mundane. But it is only in the work of one major white dramatist, Louis Nowra, that mainstream Australian theatre has offered a sustainedly penetrating and thoughtful treatment of the all-too-often repressed history of white Australia's domination of and indifference to the lives of the most dispossessed Australians.

Nowra's *The Golden Age* (1985) is, to date, the most striking and successful treatment of this theme. Though it is likely to suggest similarities and parallels with the history of Aboriginal oppression, its subject – based on historical fact – is the discovery of a lost 'clan' of white people descended from nineteenth-century convicts and gold-diggers in the rainforest of south-west Tasmania. Having decided to end their long exile and return to a society that their carefully preserved oral wisdom associates with the penal rigours of 'rack 'n' cat', the survivors are locked up in a mental asylum to avert Nazi propaganda about the threat to Aryan racial purity, the time being 1939. Here they become the objects of medical and scientific curiosity, no less callous for involving no personal cruelty. One of the doctors studying them, Archer, becomes totally obsessed with the group and especially with the daughter, Betsheb, and gradually sinks into a self-destructive and ultimately suicidal awareness of his own guilt in subjecting them to their terrible incarceration in the Hobart asylum. Nowra uses the war in Europe as an ironic commentary on the barbarity of the 'civilization' to which these 'primitive' people have returned. Francis, one of the two young men who originally found the family (and who has also fallen in love with Betsheb) returns at the end of the war profoundly disgusted and alienated by his experiences as a soldier. Tempted to kill the woman he loves (and presumably himself) to end her sufferings, he instead goes back with her to the forest where he first found her and her now dead family. The play's final image is of Betsheb's and Francis's fragile achievement of personal communion across the mental and cultural void separating them.

The Golden Age powerfully evokes a sense of the barbarity underlying Western civilization – a barbarity that has produced the horrors of fascism and European war, but also the punitive brutality of the convict system and the destruction of so many of Australia's native population. But as its title suggests, Nowra endorses rather than renounces at least one of the myths around which the intellectual culture of that civilization has long revolved. In the implicit lyricism of the family's strange version of English, and in his shaping of the ending, with Francis hoping that Betsheb 'can teach me how to see' what she sees, Nowra invites his audiences to subscribe to a myth of a golden age of communion between humans, and between humans and nature, which the alienated modern world has lost but which perhaps can be restored.

In this respect, if not in the intensity and complexity of his analysis, Nowra's play is typical of much contemporary Australian drama. For if Australia as a culture is much preoccupied by – and enamoured of – its myths and self-images, so, it must be said, are many of its dramatists. Lawler's *The Summer of the Seventeenth Doll*, Seymour's *The One Day of the Year*, Hewett's *The Man from Muckinupin*, Williamson's *Don's Party* , Gow's *Away*, Nowra's *The Golden Age*: name some of the major Australian playwrights and plays of the last three decades and you will discover, often alongside a critical commentary on some aspect of Australian reality, the celebration, implicit or explicit, of a myth perceived as in some way indispensable to it.

The lovingly ambivalent and playful manipulation of Australian national myths is a subject too large for, and not strictly relevant to, the present discussion. Its significance here is negative, in the sense that our chosen dramatist, Jack Davis, assumes much of his importance precisely because, even though the impact of white invasion and settlement was devastating for his Aboriginal forebears, he writes about the Australian historical experience of dominating and being dominated with a remarkable absence of the mythic nostalgia that afflicts even some of the best of white writing. In the violence that soon followed the initially peaceful encounters between settlers and natives the Aboriginal population was decimated. As Davis has A. O. Neville, the chief protector of Aborigines, say in his speech to the Historical Society in *No Sugar*, in the south west of Australia alone 'a people estimated to number thirteen thousand were reduced to one thousand four hundred and nineteen, of whom nearly half were half-caste' (p. 87). Elsewhere, one of Davis's characters likens the historic prison on what is now the holiday island of Rottnest, off the Western Australian coast, to 'what Auschwitz must be for the Jews', and characterizes the history of black–white relations in Australia as 'war', an 'unrecognised war of gun against spear' (*Barungin*, p. 54). In *Kullark* and the subsequent *First Born* trilogy, Jack Davis has chronicled this war, this story of genocide and oppression, from its beginnings till the present day. He has done so from an Aboriginal perspective that is never less than honest about white actions and attitudes and about the tragic effects their history has had on Aborigines in the present. Davis's small body of theatre thus constitutes an indictment of white Australian racism, a recuperation of neglected, often ignored Aboriginal history and, implicitly, a call to action by Australians black and white.

In Davis's most recent play, *Barungin (Smell the Wind*, 1988), there is an exchange between Granny Doll and her family after one of them, Shane, has played their traditional instrument, the didgeridoo:

GRANNY DOLL: (*pointing at the didgeridoo*) That's all *Nyoongahs* got now, and that don't really belong to us. Dances are gone, laws are gone, lingos just about gone, everything finished.

MEENA: Aw, Mum, things change.

PEEGUN: We got reggae, rock, soul, lots of things.

GRANNY DOLL: And grog. (p. 44)

The moment epitomizes Davis's preoccupation with the degradation of Aboriginal culture as a result of its encounter with white civilization. If the young Aborigine's preference for country music or rock, rather than his people's traditional musical culture, is one such symptom, there are others that are far more serious and damaging for black Australian communities: endemic alcoholism and drug use; high levels of violence, petty crime and imprisonment; chronic unemployment and dependence on welfare; and a sense of alienation and hopelessness that fatally erodes even the desire for individual and communal development.

Davis's realistic documenting of these ills, without false nostalgia or romanticism, is an admirable feature of his drama, requiring a great deal of courage and integrity when writing about and on behalf of a people as oppressed and historically despised as black Australians to be prepared to depict so uncompromisingly the negative features of their way of life. His commitment to documentary realism has even occasionally brought the charge that Davis has been unfaithful to the 'authentic' Aboriginal aesthetic, commonly associated with abstraction and a deep immersion in the mythic and ritualistic dimensions of Aboriginal spirituality. But if realistic representation of the harsh realities of everyday Aboriginal existence, in the past and present, is paramount in his plays, it does not mean that the evocation of the spiritual foundations of Aboriginal culture is absent. As we shall see, he shares with playwrights such as Soyinka, Walcott and Wilson a lively faith in the continuing relevance of traditional culture in confronting and representing contemporary realities, and seeking self-determination. If Davis's theatre invokes the resources of tradition rather than, as with some of the other writers, extensively exploring them, this is perhaps due as much to the urgency of his protest against immediate and extreme injustice and deprivation as to the cultural frailty of a people whose way of life has been so devastated by their historical subjugation.

The habitual setting of Davis's drama is the family living-space, whether this be an encampment in a bush clearing or a modern suburban house. In this space Davis focuses on the relations between the members of the extended Aboriginal family as they conduct their daily lives. In the chapter entitled 'Writing' in his autobiography,

Davis notes that at performances of his plays in Australia, 'Aborigines in the audience were always deeply moved to see themselves in the characters up on stage.'[2] We are now so used, as audiences of the naturalistic drama of the twentieth century, to see representations of our mundane everyday lives, faithfully conveying in minute detail the texture of social relationship and environment, that it is easy to overlook the impact and significance of a theatre that offers this experience of self-recognition to a dispossessed community for which the opportunity has not previously existed. As an 'insider', not only writing but often acting in his plays with his own Aboriginal company – some of them members of his own extended family – Davis has been able to convey faithfully the dilemmas, attitudes and values of his people in characters and action that ring true for Aboriginal audiences.

The portrait is not designed to flatter. In *The Dreamers* Dolly longs for a decent house in which to bring up her family, and her judgement on her husband Roy ('If you weren't so bloody bone tired we'd get a good 'ouse an' good furniture' (p. 76)) is entirely justified. Most of the men in Davis's plays are all too fond of sitting around drinking rather than finding work even when it's available: typically, when Dolly leaves to collect Uncle Worru from the hospital Roy, Eli and Peter proceed to spend the children's lunch money on a visit to the grog shop. Their devotion to alcohol is matched by their indulgence in deception and petty crime and their familiarity with prison culture. Peter, who gets into trouble as an eighteen-year-old in *The Dreamers* for joy-riding in a stolen car, gets out of prison in *Barungin* only to be arrested three days later for having stolen goods in his car – actually stolen by his fourteen-year-old nephew Micky – and found hanged in his cell a few hours later. Arrest and imprisonment, for Davis's characters, are a way of life, a routine fact, and the dramatist makes no attempt to conceal Aboriginal involvement in criminal activity or the negative attitudes associated with it.

Davis gives full weight to the tensions that inevitably arise in such a domestic environment. The Aboriginal family is presented as

---

[2] Jack Davis and Keith Chesson, *Jack Davis: A Life-Story*, Melbourne: Dent, 1988, p. 203.

both closely bonded and subject to recurrent internal conflict. Violence between the men, verbal or physical, is never too distant a possibility, especially – as is usually the case – when alcohol is on hand. In *Barungin* sexual tensions between Peegun and Arnie, when he returns from prison, escalate into physical violence, and Granny Doll's judgement on them ('You're all mad. Stark raving mad, the whole lot of you' (p. 51)) is fairly characteristic of the women's attitude to their quarrelsome, brawling menfolk. In the circumstances, another habitual tension is between the sexes. It is the women who typically hold the family together, often in the periodic absences of their husbands and sons. They tend also to have a greater understanding of the benefits that education and training can bring for their offspring. (An indication of the greater moral and spiritual authority of the female characters is that they are often used to give full emotional force to the valedictory quality of the plays' concluding speech or song.) When the children do enter further or higher education the problem of generational and attitudinal conflict emerges: for instance, Jamie in *Kullark* doesn't disguise his contempt for his father when he comes home from the university, though his own education doesn't stop him getting arrested.

Depressingly realistic in their presentation of the more negative features of contemporary Aboriginal life, Davis's plays also insist on its strengths and resilience. Paradoxically, it is their virtues – especially their family- and clan-based community spirit and their tolerant generosity – that contribute to the Aborigines' conflicts with white society. In *No Sugar*, for example, it is Joe's rebellious refusal to accept the confined and oppressive regime of the Moore River Native Settlement, and his love for Mary, that get him arrested and imprisoned. Tragically, it is Peegun's generous attitude to Micky that brings about Peter's arrest for carrying stolen goods in his car and his subsequent death in custody. More generally, Aboriginal values such as devotion to the extended family and to the land, even as they often provoke hostility from white Australians who do not understand or sympathize with them, help provide a certain protection, a measure of stubborn resilience and humour, which allows the characters to keep going even in the most oppressive circumstances. In *Barungin* part of the Aboriginal art of 'smelling the wind' (which is the English

meaning of the title) is to identify what prey is at hand for the hunter
to kill. Such survival skills, it's implied, are more than ever required
for urban Aborigines; and if in the play Micky's adolescent crimin-
ality is regrettable it is also understandable. As Peegun tells Shane,
who is concerned that the boy is heading for trouble: 'Bullshit, he's
just walkin' out into a big white world and he's gotta learn how to
survive. So he's learnin' – his way' (p. 29).

Effective though they are in conveying the authentic substance
of contemporary urban Aboriginal experience, Davis's plays do more
than this. In his autobiography he observes that he began working in
theatre already firmly convinced that 'writing was the best means of
influencing public opinion and bringing about an improvement in the
Aboriginal situation' (p. 191). In pursuit of this educative function,
Davis has carefully created a perspective for his presentation of the
realities of contemporary black Australian life; it is placed in the
dramatic context of a long history of Aboriginal oppression and
struggle. Taken together his four major plays constitute a radical
reinterpretation of Australian social history from an Aboriginal viewpoint, or, more accurately, a bringing to light of certain episodes in
that history of which white Australia has remained largely and
conveniently ignorant. Taken as a whole, then, Davis's dramatic
output places the contemporary condition of Aborigines in a lengthy
narrative of subjugation and implicitly invites its audiences to
consider the relationship between the main features of that history
and the current state of affairs.

His first play, *Kullark* (1979), offers a dramatic conspectus, chron-
icling crucial episodes of Western Australian Aboriginal history from
the white settlement and interweaving them with contemporary
scenes of the Yorlah family, Alec, Rosie and their son Jamie. The first
act dramatizes the earliest encounters between the settlers of the
Swan River Colony and Aborigines led by Yagan. Davis presents these
as fraught with suspicion and mutual ignorance but initially peaceful,
even extending to the barter of useful goods. The growing violence
between settlers and Aborigines is described by the Irish settler,
Alice, in her diary, as a 'tragedy': 'Lives are being lost for a mere sheep
or a bag of flour' (p. 25). Though good-natured, Will and Alice fail to

understand why Yagan and his people's judgement on the following
exchange is that *'Wetjala hartwarrah'* (white man is mad):

WILL: *(to* ALICE*)* Go and get the flour for him. *(to* YAGAN*)* If we give it
to you, it's all right, but you must not steal – sheep, pigs or bery good
[flour].
YAGAN: *(rubbing his stomach)* Tjeep kwobinyahn. (Sheep are very
good)
WILL: But the sheep belong to the white man. To the farmer.
YAGAN: *Yuart,* Wetjala kill *yonga, gwinnin, kuljuk, kalkana.*
(. . . kangaroo, duck, swan, mullet)
WILL: But all those things belong to everyone. (pp. 27–8)

With the arrival of the military and the implementation of a policy
inviting escalating violence, Davis presents the initial promise of
peaceful coexistence as doomed. The murder of Yagan – whose head
is sent to the Royal College of Surgeons for its 'phrenological interest'
– is followed by the massacre of Aborigines at Pinjarra as a warning
that the 'white man will not tolerate murder' (p. 38), and of the
authorities' condoning of sometimes large-scale as well as individual
killing of the native population as white settlement spreads south.

Alternating with these historical episodes are scenes of
present-day life in the Yorlah household somewhere in the south
west of Western Australia. Though it is a 'respectable' home, Davis
characterizes Alec as a man dependent on the bottle and the welfare
cheque. His son Jamie, on vacation from university, is critical of his
father's drinking and what he sees as his submissiveness to whites.
Alec, in turn, is hostile to the younger generation, especially those,
like his son, who seem to be coming under the influence of whites
because of their education. In the course of act two, which again
takes us back in time to focus on the Yorlah household through the
depression of the thirties and the postwar years, the audience is given
an insight into why Alec behaves and thinks as he does. We see how
during the depression years (which were particularly hard ones for
Aborigines) Alec's parents Thomas and Mary Yorlah, and their two
children, are rounded up and dumped in the desolate Moore River
Settlement. The adult Alec returns from war service with high hopes
and 'citizenship rights', which technically classifies him as white,

only to be warned by his (white) commanding officer that 'Australia is still a racist country' in which he will have to 'try harder, do better, prove yourself more than a white man' (p. 58). The truth of this is immediately demonstrated when Alec is harassed by a local white policeman, who is only looking for an opportunity to arrest him. Ironically, his exemption from the Natives Administration Act could give the policeman his chance, since it requires Alec to stay away from the reserve and members of his extended family who are not exempted – thus enforcing a kind of *de facto* apartheid. But the still young and hopeful Alec is ambitious for his children: 'I want 'em to grow up to be teachers or nurses, something with a bit of dignity. They've been servants and farm hands far too long. Far too long' (p. 64)

This intimation of the attitudes and legislation at work in Australian society, which have reduced Alec from his optimistic younger self to the object of his son's criticism, is counterpointed in act two by the latter's exposure to some of those forces, which are still operating and which can still personally affect him, in spite of his education. Jamie encounters white racism in the person of the local publican, who taunts him with involvement in the theft of alcohol from his premises, to which the young man responds by throwing beer in his face. After his court appearance, which results in his being bound over for a year, Jamie has a new tone towards, and implicitly a better understanding of, his father: 'You know, Dad, today everything in that courthouse was white. White walls, white judge ... only one black spot in there ... no, three – me in the box and you two up in the gallery. Yeah, it's an awful bloody feelin' all up there on your own' (p. 65). If he has now been initiated in the truth about having to live in a white man's world, he also discovers another, pleasanter one: that it is possible to use age-old Aboriginal survival instincts to get at least something of what one wants. Alec produces a bottle for a celebratory drink, replying to Jamie's 'You sly ol' fox, where'd you get that?' with a cheerfully enigmatic 'You gotta be tough in this world, son, you gotta be tough' (p. 65).

Written for performance in a variety of venues, including schools as part of a Theatre in Education (TIE) programme, the play requires relatively simple methods of staging while suggesting a broad sweep of time and place. *Kullark* exploits the possibilities of music and spectacle in simple but effective ways. For example, as well as indicating distinctions of time, the different kinds of music used reinforce the loss of traditional Aboriginal culture, the country-and-western introducing the contemporary scenes contrasting with Yagan's chant and dance in act one, scene two, when he invokes Warrgul the Rainbow Serpent (for Aborigines, the creator and guarantor of the earth and life). Similarly, Warrgul retains an emblematic visual presence during the performance of the play through the painting of the Rainbow Serpent in the shape of a map of the Swan River. But when the invading white characters enter they do so through revolving screens that 'cut' segments of the Serpent and replace it with European images of Australia. By such means, together with the alternation of scenes between the past and present day, Davis is able to convey the continuity of white Australian racism and its effects on Aborigines, but also the history of black resistance and its spiritual basis.

Davis's next play, *The Dreamers* (1983), the first part of his *First Born* trilogy, concentrates on another contemporary Western Australian Aboriginal family, the Wallitches. The dramatic focus is on Uncle Worru, who is brought back from hospital to live out his last few months with his family. On his better days the old man likes to drink and spin yarns about the old times; but as he grows more senile and rambling his mind becomes locked in memory and imagining, projected for us by images of the tribal family and the Dancer. Through its interplay of present-day domestic scenes and those in Worru's mind, *The Dreamers* evokes the pathos of an individual life and a whole people degraded by their dispossession.

The effects of that dispossession are evident enough in the Wallitch household. The men, apart from Robert, are chronically unemployed, their energy mainly devoted to drinking, quarrelling, living off social security and occasional begging. Peter, the elder son, is arrested and imprisoned in the course of the play, going the way of most of his older male relatives. The younger members of the family, Shane and Meena, are losing their *Nyoongah* language and culture; Meena, contrary to her mother Dolly's wishes, wants to leave school and is already in the habit of coming home very late at night. Not that the picture is one of unrelieved misery: Davis's sense of truth as a dramatist allows him to present the negatives and at the same time convey the humour and warmth of the family, and the resourcefulness of at least some of its members, namely Dolly and her nephew Robert.

The dominant emotional tone of *The Dreamers*, however, is elegiac: a lament for a tribal past, for a people once physically and spiritually in harmony with their world and now lost in an alien environment. The loss is eloquently demonstrated in the first act when Worru, only just out of hospital and on medication, gets drunk with the other men and to the accompaniment of disco music embarks on '*a drunken stumbling version of a half-remembered tribal dance ... until his feet tangle and he falls heavily*' (p. 86). The scene ends with a freeze, a lighting change and the replacement of the disco music by the sound of the didgeridoo and clap sticks: the intricately painted Dancer appears against a red sky, dancing downstage and across in front of the contemporary characters, his feet pounding into the stage, before dancing back to his starting point and disappearing in darkness. In this and the other scenes of Worru's 'dreaming' the almost lost world of the tribal past is made a palpable reality. The contrast with the prevailing urban squalor could hardly be more bleak. The point is made explicit in Dolly's valedictory speech, which concludes the play, as she recalls the young Worru 'straight as wattle spears', displaying his prowess as a hunter when 'he looked like a king in the sun' (pp. 138–9).

The dramatic impact generated by the play's structure as an extended counterpoint between the realistic scenes of contemporary life and the stylized enactment of the images in old Worru's mind ('and my longing is an echo / a re-occurring dream') can be conveyed theatrically by creating two distinct 'worlds' on the stage. This was what was done, by Davis's account very effectively, when *The Dreamers* was performed at the Sydney Opera House and on a tour of the eastern states of Australia. The Aboriginal painter Shane Pickett was commissioned to design dye-and-gauze abstracts depicting Warrgul the Rainbow Serpent and his journey along the Swan River to reach the sea at what is now Fremantle. With the aid of these abstracts and lighting effects, the stage space could signify both the contemporary and the tribal world, but with 'an interplay between the past, which could emerge from a shadow behind the gauze to become a reality, and the present'.[3]

In the second play of the trilogy, *No Sugar* (1985), Davis concentrates his attention on the depression years following the Wall Street crash of 1929. This was a particularly hard time in Western Australia, but for Aborigines it brought exceptional oppression and suffering. Moreover, for reasons of political expediency in an election year it was decided by the white state authorities to round up the native population of Northam and transfer them to the hated Moore River Settlement, where Davis himself spent several years of his youth. *No Sugar* follows the enforced migration of the Millimurra family, and the tribulations and eventually successful struggle of Joe and his lover Mary to escape from the settlement and gain some kind of freedom.

The play is most effective as a dramatized exposé of white Australian racist ideology and the cruelty of actions sanctioned by 'paternalist' official policy. Davis is not afraid to dramatize the words and behaviour of real historical figures such as A. O. Neville, the chief protector of Aborigines, and Mr Neal, the superintendent of the Moore River Settlement. Neville, in his address to the Historical Society (act three, scene five), speaks of 'that little band of pioneers' who first anchored in the Swan River, 'little knowing that they faced in the fertile valleys of the South-West alone some thirteen thousand savages' (p. 85). Though he is honest in acknowledging, at the end of his speech, the genocide of the Aboriginal population in this area, Neville is represented as firmly committed to a paternalist view of race relations. On his Australia Day visit to the settlement he tells the Millimurras and others that

> you are preparing yourselves here to take your place in
> Australian society, to live as other Australians live, and to live
> alongside other Australians; to learn to enjoy the privileges and
> to shoulder the responsibilities of living like the white man, to
> be treated equally, not worse, not better, under the law. (p. 97)

[3] *Ibid.*, p. 200.

He is horrified when the Aborigines subvert the singing of the hymn 'There is a Happy Land' with a parody that sums up their true situation:

> There is a happy land,
> Far, far away.
> No sugar in our tea,
> Bread and butter we never see.
> That's why we're gradually
> Fading away. (p. 98)

He regards it as a 'disgraceful demonstration of ingratitude', since he believes his own rhetoric about the 'fortunate' Aborigines 'in this small corner of the Empire ... being provided for with adequate food and shelter' (p. 97).

Neville's spitefulness in punishing them for their act of subversion by withdrawing their 'privileges' ('there will be no Christmas this year!') is outdone by the sustained cruelty to and abuse of his charges perpetrated by the settlement superintendent, Neal. Davis presents Neal as a man who, having practised his racism on the blacks of South Africa, relishes his opportunities to brutalize black Australians – and especially to sexually abuse the Aboriginal girls. He is a drinker, a lecher and a cowardly sadist, a man totally devoid of any kind of constructive vision of the welfare of his charges. He even comes into conflict with his colleague, Sister Eileen, over her desire to start a small library, because he believes that 'there's enough troublemakers without giving them ideas' (p. 96). On the other hand Sister Eileen and Neal's wife, Matron, represent the acceptable face of white paternalism, blinkered by their unquestioning acceptance of a fundamentally racist ideology but genuinely decent and well-meaning. One of the main elements of this ideology is Christianity, which in its positive aspect motivates Sister Eileen and her kind. But *No Sugar* asserts that a society which considers itself Christian not only hypocritically violates its own tenets in its treatment of Aborigines, but even behaves in ways comparable to the biblical enemies of the early Christians. The point is made by calling the Aboriginal hero and heroine, who try to escape persecution, Joe and Mary; and by having Sister Eileen tell the story of Herod's slaughter of the innocents at her Sunday School; and by dramatically relating this to Mary's fear that she will lose her baby by Joe if she allows it out of her sight, which is based on the actual practices of (legally) abducting Aboriginal children, and the not uncommon killing of infants fathered by whites on black women.

Christianity also has a significant presence in *Barungin*, which takes the story of the Wallitch family on into the next generation. The play begins and ends with a funeral service, Eli's at the beginning and Peter's, after his death in police custody, at the end. Davis presents the negative side of Christianity as an American fundament-alist preacher drones on interminably about renouncing the ways of the flesh, an injunction which has the Aboriginal mourners looking quizzically at one another and at the audience. Its more positive side is embodied in Robert, who – like Davis himself – combines his faith with an insider's knowledge of and activist concern for Aboriginal culture and civil rights. In act two, scene four, just before he makes his speech at the Rotary club, Robert articulates what seems to be the author's essentially hopeful and Christian-influenced view of the way forward:

ARNIE: You stir 'em up, Robert. Make them *wetjalas* piss.

MEENA: You can't hurt *wetjalas*; they've got no conscience.

ROBERT: Yes they have. We just gotta help them find it.

PETER: There hasn't been much sign of it in the last two hundred years.

MEENA: And there won't be in the next two hundred.

ROBERT: You're wrong.

PETER: Ah, all black fellas are good for is fightin' amongst themselves.

ROBERT: You're wrong. (p. 52)

His speech is, precisely, an attempt to stir up that conscience among an influential section of the white population by educating it about the lengthy history of Aboriginal deaths in custody. But only a few hours after he has done so he has to tell his own family that one of its members has died in a police cell.

Barungin dramatizes the burning contemporary issue for black and other concerned Australians – the continuing scandal of Aboriginal deaths in custody. It combines the optimistic spirit of Robert's appeal to white conscience with great anger and frustration at the latest episodes in a history almost as long as white colonialism itself: as Robert points out in his speech, the first recorded Aboriginal deaths in custody date from 1832. The force of the anger is all the greater for Davis's eschewal of overtly emotional speeches or moralizing. Instead, he carefully juxtaposes scenes and devices that, taken together, certainly created an electrifyingly strong impact when the play had its premiere in Perth in 1988. The scene in which Robert announces the death to his family is followed by the voice-over, in the darkness, of the coroner's report, with its detailed, scientifically neutral tone: and this is, in turn, followed by the final scene, at the graveside, in which the actors place wreaths as Meena reads a list of names of those who have died in custody, from the beginning up to the latest, John Pat, whose death occurred in a police cell after an alleged fight with four officers shortly before the play was produced. Linking these concluding scenes is the silent image of the tribal Dancer, his movement across the stage accompanied by the haunting sound of the didgeridoo. In its final moments the theatrical illusion of *Barungin* blurs into the most urgently topical actuality: black actors who have presented a dramatic fiction to an audience become black people enacting a symbolic ceremony of mourning and protest against their continuing oppression before their fellow citizens, white and black.

Davis's pioneering work as a playwright, actor, poet and all-round social activist on behalf of Aboriginal rights has made him a father-figure and an inspiration for younger Aboriginal writers and performers such as Richard Walley and Bob Maza. It is in large part due to his success that other, younger Aboriginal playwrights have received some recognition; though this is not to discount others, such as Robert Merritt, whose *The Cake Man* was the first Aboriginal play to be successful in the mainstream Australian theatre. It does not seem fanciful to believe that Davis's and his younger Aboriginal colleagues' theatrical efforts have had some effect, however small, in creating a climate in which the Australian prime minister, Paul Keating, has belatedly but importantly made a formal acknowledgement of the atrocities committed against Aboriginal Australians. But while white Australian attitudes towards Aborigines are changing, and though the Australian theatre has found some room to accommodate black Australian artists, it cannot be said that Davis's clear-eyed and penetratingly honest reappraisal of Australian social history from an Aboriginal perspective has, as yet, done as much as one hopes it still may to disturb the nostalgic, myth-laden account so beloved of so many white Australians, including some of its leading dramatists.

Wole Soyinka and the Nigerian theatre of ritual vision

Since receiving their independence in the 1950s and early 1960s, the countries of sub-Saharan Africa have earned an unenviable reputation as a collective continental basket-case. The crisis in Rwanda, which is occurring as this is written, is only the latest and, sadly, the greatest in a long succession that now includes innumerable civil wars, large-scale social strife, catastrophes such as famine and drought, disease on an epidemic scale, and, as a constant backdrop, apparently unvanquishable economic stagnation and political instability and oppression.

The reasons for, and consequences of, African 'backwardness' are complex and debatable, but few, surely, would now dissent from the view that Africa's colonial past continues to be a determining factor in the ills that beset it in the present. For it is evident enough that, whatever the failings for which African governments and ruling elites are largely or exclusively responsible, the disruption of African history by the European imperial powers has created a range of political, economic and cultural problems of enormous magnitude. Borders were artificially imposed, nations created and named by imperial fiat. Peoples of different language and culture, often knowing – or wishing to know – little or nothing of each other, were forcibly yoked together and, when it was decided in distant capitals that the winds of change were blowing in a direction that pointed to political independence, were expected henceforth to behave as if they had organically evolved as liberal capitalist democracies.[1]

[1]   Except, of course, in those countries such as Angola and Mozambique, which belonged to an imperial power, Portugal, that refused to yield its colonial empire, thus instigating long and bloody liberation wars.

Torn by ethnic rivalry, their economies drastically modified under colonialism to fit the imperatives of the imperialist economic world order, and saddled under neocolonialism by mounting foreign debt, large-scale corruption and the usual accompaniments of 'under-development', it is hardly surprising that so many African countries have failed to offer even the minimum acceptable standards of living or opportunities for a decent life to the majority of their people. In such circumstances it would be unrealistic to expect the arts to flourish, though, miraculously, they sometimes have. When they have, it has only been by overcoming the obstacles presented by the chronic lack of financial support, inadequate physical resources, and – at least in the case of that most public of arts, the theatre – the threat and sometimes the reality of censorship. If the continent – excluding for the moment the special case of South Africa – can boast a wide range of theatre, and a drama created by writers as diverse as Hubert Ogunde, Ama Ata Aidoo, Ngugi wa Thiong'o and his collaborators, Ebrahim Hussein, Ola Rotimi and, pre-eminently, Wole Soyinka, it has to be said that much remains to be done to create a theatrical profession willing and able to make and perform a repertoire of 'serious' drama for an appreciative audience.

In spite of both these immediate difficulties and the broader cultural impact of the historical disruption of African cultures, dramatists in Africa, like its artists in general, enjoy at least one crucial advantage over their black counterparts in America, the West Indies or Australia. This is the fact that colonialist intervention, which obviously varied in its scope and effects over the continent, mainly failed – even where it attempted – to destroy the traditional arts of the colonized. Indigenous performance traditions over most of the continent have remained healthily intact, and often flourish at the popular, community level such as in the celebration of seasonal rituals, in folk theatre and in such primarily urban, travelling theatre as that of Hubert Ogunde and Baba Sala or the Ghanaian Concert Party. The riches of the oral tradition are available to African playwrights as to Caribbean or Aboriginal, and have been widely and successfully exploited, notably in J. P. Clark's *Ozidi* and Efua Sutherland's *The Marriage of Anansewa*. Like dramatists of colonized or subordinated cultures elsewhere, African writers have also been concerned to recuperate and reinterpret their own histories, with varying ideological effects and in differing formal styles; for example, in Ola Rotimi's *Ovonramwen Nogbaisi*, Ebrahim Hussein's *Kinjeketile* and Ngugi wa Thiong'o and Micere Mugo's *The Trial of Dedan Kimathi*. But whereas the dramatist of a subordinated culture often has only a tenuous and problematic relationship with the theatrical traditions of his or her people's past, for the African playwright the full resources of tradition are usually available, to be used (or rejected) alongside European models.

In this respect, at least, what many modern theatre practitioners have eagerly and not always successfully sought for, the African dramatist has been able to take more or less for granted. In Europe and America writers, actors and directors, of whom Genet, Grotowski, Beck and Brook are only some of the most notable, have for decades looked to other cultures for models and inspiration for a ritually based, 'metaphysical' theatre. Among black Americans, especially the advocates in the last thirty years or so of a militant and 'separatist' theatre, there has been much discussion of a distinctively Afro-American aesthetic. In the Caribbean, too, theatre artists have often sought a 'return' to African roots in form and style. Whatever one's opinion of the success of such projects, the mere fact of the theorizing and experimenting that has initiated and accompanied them indicates the extent to which they have had to be aspired to as desirable but essentially alien ideals, rather than appropriated in the course of an organic development. In Africa, on the other hand, the inherited Western dramaturgical and performance models have more often than not, at least in the more interesting drama, been fused with familiar, living traditions drawn from ritual and popular theatres, religious and secular, of the African peoples.

No African dramatist has wrought such fusions more often, in such prolific stylistic variety, or to greater intellectual and aesthetic effect, than the Nigerian Yoruba playwright, poet, novelist and political activist, Wole Soyinka. Soyinka was educated both in Nigeria and England (at Ibadan and Leeds Universities), and he has been profoundly influenced by his acquaintance with both his native African and Euro-American theatres (in the fifties he was one of the illustrious band who served some of their dramatic apprenticeship at

London's Royal Court Theatre). At the same time, while familiar
with both cultures, he has long been preoccupied by the West's
disruptive effect on the African continent and in particular his own
country of Nigeria. But in only one of his plays does he directly
dramatize the issue, in ways that reveal both the remarkable dramatic
power in his capacity to blend European dramaturgy with ritually
based theatrical performance and the characteristic quality of his
thinking about the distinctive nature of Yoruba (Soyinka would
probably say African) reality.

Death and the King's Horseman (1976) is based on real events in Oyo,
western Nigeria, in 1945. The British colonial officer Pilkings intervenes in the ritual suicide of the king's horseman, Elesin Oba, causing
him to fail in his duty to follow his lord, the Alafin, into the ancestor
world. Eventually Elesin does manage to kill himself while held in
custody by the British authorities, but not before his son Olunde, who
has returned from his medical studies in Britain on hearing of the
crisis, sacrifices himself in his stead to try to ensure the continued
spiritual wellbeing of his community. Whether Olunde's act is
sufficient to redeem his father's failure is uncertain: as the Praise
Singer tells Elesin before his death, 'Our world is tumbling in the void
of strangers', and there is no guarantee of what the end will be.

Ritual pervades *Death and the King's Horseman*. The scenes
of Elesin in the marketplace with the women have a lyrical, incantatory quality about them, as he prepares, and is prepared, for his
ceremonial death. The dancing, the music, the richly metaphorical
and incantatory language, the Praise Singer's and women's exaltation
of Elesin and their dressing of him in resplendent robes, all of these
create a 'magical', ritualistic effect for characters and audience alike.
But the ritualism takes an unexpected turn – almost, for a few
moments, stalls altogether – when Elesin sights the beautiful young
woman betrothed to Iyaloja's son. His desire for his seed to 'take
root / In the earth of my choice' is however accommodated, even if
there is still a discordant note in Elesin's exasperation at Iyaloja's
blunt reminder to him that the same hands which 'prepare your
bridal chamber' will also lay his shrouds (p. 162).

The next time Elesin appears (in scene three), the ritualistic action continues and is intensified. He hands Iyaloja the white cloth stained with his new bride's virgin blood and then, to the accompaniment of the drums, the Praise Singer's exhortations and the women's dirge, he begins to dance out of this life into the next. By the fading of the lights at the end of the scene Elesin Oba is deep in trance, on the very verge of that passage between the different realms of being which Soyinka calls the gulf of transition. But as the structure of the play makes clear, alternating as it does between the scenes involving Elesin and those featuring the colonial authorities, there is close at hand another attitude, another view of life, that is not only different but uncomprehending and hostile to the ritual events proceeding in the marketplace. Soyinka makes the point even sharper by using dance and festivity – the tango and the fancy dress ball – in the 'colonial' scenes as an ironic contrast to Elesin and his retinue's ritual dancing. Not only is the tango that Pilkings and his wife are dancing when first seen a frivolous, superficial form of dance compared to that in the marketplace, but its exponents are presented, in a none too subtle piece of satire, as being so ignorant and contemptuous of indigenous culture that they happily desecrate it by wearing egungun masquerade costumes as fancy dress. The attitudes underlying this display of sacrilege are evident in Pilkings's reaction to his constable's report that Elesin Oba 'is to commit death tonight as a result of native custom' (p. 166). First, he jumps to the conclusion that Elesin is going to commit ritual murder; and then, when he learns the truth, he puts it all down to 'some barbaric custom' and decides to have Elesin locked up. At no point does Pilkings, or his somewhat more intelligent and culturally sensitive wife Jane, consider the possible significance of the ritual event or their intervention in it.

Soyinka extends the comparison, and the satire, through the dance sequence at the beginning of scene four, which takes poetic licence so far as to present a British prince gracing the local European club with his royal presence as he makes a wartime tour of the colonies. The point is made, specifically by the returned Olunde in his exchange with Jane in scene four, that Elesin and the Prince are engaged on similar tasks: if the former is performing the trance-dance that will take him into the ancestor world so as to secure the wellbeing of his people, the Prince's tour, with its ceremonial music and dancing, is designed to keep up morale among his subjects. Elesin's action is presented as being deeply rooted in an organic culture that knows the meaning and value of its rituals. The colonialists, on the other hand, while being horrified at what they can only understand as native barbarism, fail to recognize that they are ritualists too (the Prince's visit), and are themselves embroiled in actions that others might find senseless and barbaric. Again it is Olunde who functions as the play's *raisonneur*, making the point about the massive disaster that is the white peoples' war, and commenting on Jane's story (about the captain who blew himself up with his ship in the local harbour rather than risk harm to others) by pointing to its 'affirmative' quality, analogous with his father's action.

Olunde's confidence in the successful outcome of that action is, however, misplaced. But the reason for Elesin's failure to complete the ritual is more complicated than Pilkings's mere intervention, as the Oba acknowledges to his young bride: 'For I confess to you, daughter, my weakness came not merely from the abomination of the white man who came violently into my fading presence, there was also a weight of longing on my earth-held limbs' (p. 207). And this weight, he concedes, had to do with his longing for his new wife being 'more than a desire of the flesh': 'You were the final gift of the living to their emissary to the land of the ancestors, and perhaps your warmth and youth brought new insights of this world to me and turned my feet leaden on this side of the abyss' (p. 207).

But there is more to it even than this, as Elesin, a few minutes later, tries to explain to the angry Iyaloja, who reminds him of the warnings she had uttered when he was first distracted by the sight of the young woman in the marketplace:

What were warnings beside the moist contact of living earth between my fingers? What were warnings beside the renewal of famished embers lodged eternally in the heart of man. But even that, even if it overwhelmed one with a thousand fold temptations to linger a little while, a man could overcome it. It is when the alien hand pollutes the source of will, when a stranger force of violence shatters the mind's calm resolution,

this is when a man is made to commit the awful treachery of
relief, commit in his thought the unspeakable blasphemy of
seeing the hand of the gods in this alien rupture of his world. I
know it was this thought that killed me, sapped my powers and
turned me into an infant in the hands of unnameable strangers.
(pp. 211–12)

Ultimately, then, it is not Elesin's own vitality and love of life
that has undone him, nor even, it seems, the physical force exercised
by the colonial authorities. It is something in his own mind, the
'blasphemous' thought that in some way the gods have condoned the
colonialists' intervention in his ritual action. And this is a thought, at
least in Elesin's account, that proceeds from a mental 'pollution'
which corrupts the will. There is no reason to believe that Elesin's
version is intended as a self-deception, and it seems to square with a
comment Soyinka makes in his 'author's note' to the printed text of
his play: 'The Colonial Factor is an incident, a catalytic incident
merely. The confrontation in the play is largely metaphysical,
contained in the human vehicle which is Elesin and the universe of
the Yoruba mind . . .' (p. 145). Crucial as Pilkings's intervention is, it
is not what most concerns Soyinka. What does is the capacity of
colonialism to undermine psychologically those charged with ensuring the wellbeing and continuity of the culture. The necessary ritual
action is finally performed; but whether it can now be effective is
uncertain. Certainly the Praise Singer's gloss on events, and judgement of Elesin, are harsh:

> Elesin, we placed the reins of the world in your hands yet you
> watched it plunge over the edge of the bitter precipice. You sat
> with folded arms while evil strangers tilted the world from its
> course and crashed it beyond the edge of emptiness – you
> muttered, there is little one man can do, you left us floundering
> in a blind future. Your heir has taken the burden on himself.
> What the end will be, we are not gods to tell. But this young
> shoot has poured its sap into the parent stalk, and we know this
> is not the way of life. Our world is tumbling in the void of
> strangers, Elesin. (p. 218)

Iyaloja, who has the authority of tradition on her side, counsels the young widow to turn her mind to the unborn child it is assumed she has conceived by Elesin. There is no hope in the present, the play suggests; but perhaps Olunde's sacrifice, and his father's belated entrance into the passage of transition, may yet bear fruit.

Death and the King's Horseman has proved popular with Western playgoers and readers, being regularly produced and featuring on many syllabi. This is probably because it is one of this 'difficult' dramatist's more accessible plays, with its dramatization of British colonialism in Nigeria, its British characters (even if they are stereotypes) and its theatrically exciting use of music, dance and trance ritual in the marketplace scenes. If its interest for Western audiences has been exceptional, its basic structure and underlying preoccupation are nevertheless characteristic of Soyinka's drama as a whole. As with so many of his plays, it is built around a ritual action, presented as profoundly important for the wellbeing of a community, which is impaired or prevented, and which leaves the characters and audience in uncertainty about the consequences for the future.

If colonialism is the immediate cause of the interruption – and perhaps fatal impairment – of the ritual in *Death and the King's Horseman*, Soyinka's drama offers, over the years, many other forces operating to pervert or weaken ritual efficacy. In *A Dance of the Forests* (1960), shown during the Nigerian Independence Day celebrations, the ritual gathering of the tribes – apparently modelled on a Yoruba New Year festival – is flawed by the general refusal of the living human community to recognize and accept the visitors from the world of the dead, and by the desire to rewrite history to omit such inglorious interludes of indigenous tyranny as the reign of Mata Kharibu. Such abuse of power, this time by a modern African leader, is also the reason for the perversion of the Festival of the New Yam in *Kongi's Harvest* (1965), in which Kongi seeks to glorify himself and reinforce his tyranny by blasphemously presenting himself as the Spirit of the Harvest. The purification ritual in which the hero of *The Strong Breed* (1964) eventually becomes involved is initially invalidated by the community's practice of selecting an unwilling outsider as their sacrificial 'carrier' rather than a properly qualified 'strong breed' ritualist who can endure, like the Old Man, the arduous task assigned him. In *The Road* (1965), perhaps Soyinka's most enigmatic play, the interruption of the ritual seems to be due to mere chance, as Kotonu, having escaped death at the rotten bridge by 'a miracle', drives his mammy wagon into the drivers' festival in honour of the god Ogun and knocks down Murano as he dances possessed as an egungun.

Many if not all these forces, which in some way prevent or impair ritual potency, may be grouped together as manifestations of the desire for power. This is a theme on which Soyinka has spoken and written eloquently, and on which his disagreements with his left-wing Nigerian critics have largely turned. In his inaugural lecture as a professor at the University of Ife, Soyinka argues that his radical opponents have failed to confront adequately the problem of power because it 'cannot be quantified or reduced to the language of historicism: it stands outside history'. Power, he argues, is an enormous embarrassment for the Marxist left, for while it is true that 'the motive force of social transformation does exist within the realm of socio-economics', power has proved a durable and autonomous partner in the transformation of history, cutting across the imperatives of race, creed, class and ideology. The function of literature and art is to attempt to contain and control these 'anti-humanistic malformations', which are produced by the will to power.

Colonialism, then, is only one form of what Soyinka seems to see as the omnivorous, deforming will to power on the African continent. It is an impulse that he has dramatized from his earliest writing for the stage. In the early tragedies the exercise of power is associated with the embodiments or representatives of their communities and its orthodox wisdom, who are challenged by youthful rebels. The Kadiye of *The Swamp Dwellers* (1959) and Isola's reverend father in *Camwood on the Leaves* (1965) are both authority figures, associated with the established power structure in their societies, who oppress and destroy the wellbeing of others. Their youthful antagonists are defeated: Igwesu, alienated from both his home in the swamps and the distant city in which he has lived, ends in despair, and Isola's revolt against his father's authoritarianism leads him to murder.

But these two early tragedies at least hint at a potentially fruitful association between the vitality of youth and the resources of tradition: in *The Swamp Dwellers* through the mysterious figure of the blind beggar, with his faith in his 'healer's hands', who makes himself Igwesu's bondsman and remains to work the land; and in *Camwood on the Leaves* through Isola's symbolic association with the ritual figure of the egungun.

The still tentative linking of Isola with traditional ritual practice and wisdom is more fully worked out in *A Dance of the Forests* and *The Strong Breed*, through the characters of Demoke and Eman. In the former, a play suffused with ritualistic action, Demoke the artist, assisted by the god Ogun (who here makes his only appearance as a dramatic character in Soyinka's work), intervenes to prevent Eshuoro, the powerful antagonist of humanity and Ogun, from claiming the Half-Child, the symbolic victim of the cycle of human 'cannibalism' that the play identifies, through the 'flashback' to the court of Mata Kharibu, as an intrinsic feature of African history and its legacy of political tyranny. His daring action forces him to climb the totem he has carved especially for the feast of the Gathering of the Tribes, the sacrificial basket clamped on his head by Eshuoro's jester. Though there is much that is obscure and perplexing in this fascinating but difficult play, it seems that in the course of the ritualistic 'dance', which dominates its second half, Demoke re-enacts Ogun's progress through the gulf of transition and that, in doing so, he moves towards a personal redemption for his crime in murdering his apprentice Oremole. There is also a deliberately ambivlent suggestion that Demoke's sacrifice may initiate a new 'self-apprehension' for everyone: even Rola, the notorious Madame Tortoise, emerges chastened from her experience, though, as Agboreko the elder says, 'We paid dearly for this wisdom newly acquired.' When he climbs as ritual sacrifice to the top of the totem, Demoke may be understood as overcoming not only his vertigo – the cause of his violence on Oremole – but his fear of the abyss and the dark forces this fear inspired within him. His triumphant climb and fall, which is broken by Ogun, signals the overthrow of the apparently victorious Eshuoro and the other antagonists of the values embodied by Ogun.

In the context of Nigeria's Independence Day celebrations,

Soyinka seems to have been insisting that a truly humane modern state can only emerge from a collective recognition of the real historical inheritance and a visionary transformation of it, accomplished through the bringing together of past, present and future in a moment of ritual 'vision'. The living want the Gathering of the Tribes to be a glorification of the past, and they are angry when their guests from the ancestor world turn out to be reminders of the inheritance of brutality and evil.

The Strong Breed is on the face of it a much simpler and more accessible play, delivering a similar statement about a community's self-deception and perversion of its ritual activity. But a detailed reading reveals it as actually one of Soyinka's most secretive texts, with its intimations of an interior drama played out in the author's imagination that is not made fully explicit at the surface level. The air of mystery, of an unnamed evil and an inexplicable inherited destiny, are, of course, parts of the conscious dramatic effect. But there are other mysteries that are never clarified. Why does its redeemer-hero, Eman, so definitively reject his inherited function as sacrificial 'carrier'? And what is the nature of the 'strange knowledge' he sought at the 'vain shrine of secret strength'? There are no answers to such questions as part of the overt meaning of the play, just as there is no obvious answer to the problem of the ultimate value that Eman's sacrificial death has for the community.

What is clear, however, is that, like Demoke in *A Dance of the Forests*, the protagonist of *The Strong Breed* achieves his ritual act of attempted communal redemption for reasons that are complexly personal and which in his case involve a resolute attempt to avoid the very role that he ultimately finds himself playing. Eman is the outsider *par excellence* in voluntary exile from his own home, living in a community where he has at best been only grudgingly accepted and is still deeply distrusted. He acts in fatal opposition to the power of Oroge and Jaguna as leaders and interpreters of the orthodox belief and practice of their community. But he does so only after a crisis in which he discovers his real identity and necessary vocation. And this discovery only occurs because he has severed himself from the inherited values of his society – symbolized by his abrupt departure in the middle of his initiation – and has rejected his father's calling as a suitable vocation for himself. He finally achieves his maturity, not through the unquestioning acceptance of traditional values and his strong-breed inheritance, but through his resolve to take the solitary way in search of a personally apprehended truth. His decision to take Ifada's place as sacrificial carrier is the product of his disinterested compassion, even for those who are not his own kind, which is itself the fruit of his lonely wandering and suffering.

We have seen that Soyinka, in his non-dramatic writing, advocates traditional wisdom and its expression in ritual practice as the primary means by which to resist the deformation of African culture by colonialism and its post-colonial legacy. In these early plays he explores some of the implications of this fundamental belief, in ways that obviously have personal connections with his development as an artist towards imaginative maturity and a full realization of his humanistic, visionary vocation. What is most striking is his uncompromising assertion of the paradoxical relationship between tradition and the individual. The protagonist charged with the performance of the ritual act, which may redeem a society, can only do so by means of the traditional wisdom and its customary practices; but it seems that the resources of tradition can only be gained through an heroically individualist experience of personal self-discovery and self-renewal, which at least initially involves rebellion against and even exile from the traditional culture. In these plays of his early maturity, Soyinka may be seen as dramatizing his own experience, and perhaps that of other young African intellectuals whose education and aspirations were forcing them to question their personal relationships with their culture, traditional and modern.

The Road seems to be much less a record of vocational preoccupations than *A Dance of the Forests* and *The Strong Breed*, and its intensely metaphysical preoccupations arguably set it apart from his other tragedies. The doubts and uncertainties that have so far been reserved for treatment of the potency of visionary ritual action as the means to collective redemption, are now extended to the search for visionary experience itself. More so than the earlier plays, then, *The Road* is marked by a pervasive ambivalence that seems to compel the audience into a certain tragi-comic detachment; and at the centre of this ambivalence is the figure of Professor.

Soyinka deliberately prevents us from knowing exactly what to make of Professor. He is at the same time a recognizable Nigerian 'comic type' – the word-besotted though formally uneducated eccentric whose mind has been somewhat turned by his 'learning' – and a genuinely charismatic character, the (at least arguably) authentic seeker after strange knowledge and power. Significantly, when he first appears he is in what a stage direction describes as a *'high state of excitement'*, muttering to himself of miracles, but he is persuaded by Samson that he has missed his way. Professor is ready to believe it: 'Indeed anything is possible when I pursue the Word' (p. 157). The moment is nicely emblematic of the complexity of visionary questing, both for the character and his audience. Professor is indeed in the right place, but has been deceived by appearances; on the other hand, having 'sight and vision only for the Word' (p. 153), he is quite likely to lose his way, as he himself admits. Throughout the play the audience is caught in the tension epitomized in this moment – the tension between a commonsense view that plots Professor's progress on a map of comic or tragi-comic folly, and an acceptance of the authenticity of his intimations of visionary enlightenment, with their tragic implications. The climax of the developing tension is Professor's murder, by Say Tokyo Kid, and his final speech, which seems to encapsulate his accumulated wisdom and to offer the key to how the nature and value of his quest are to be assessed.

Professor has sought the Word in many and various contexts, but his ultimate goal is constant: he is searching for a vicarious experience of the passage from life to death in the belief that 'the Word may be found companion not to life, but Death' (p. 159). He hopes thus to discover, in death, the secret of life's meaning and thereby 'cheat fear, by foreknowledge' (p. 227). As Murano begins his god-possessed climactic dance, Professor – who 'cannot yet believe that death's revelation must be total, or not at all' (p. 226) – speaks of his elation at the prospect of at last having the ultimate secret revealed to him:

> I feel powered tonight, but that is usual. But I also feel at last a true excitement of the mind and spirit. As if that day has been lowered at last which I have long awaited. Surely I am not

alone. If I am that, then I have wasted evenings of instruction on you. (*Mildly, almost with tiredness.*) You dregs, you emptied faces, have I shared my thoughts with you for nothing? (p. 227)

The possibility that he has all along been misguided in at least part of his endeavour – the instruction of others in the spiritual mysteries – is explicit. Immediately following these words, Say Tokyo Kid shouts 'Stop it! Stop It! ... I say stop playing along with this sacrilege' (p. 227). Death is now in their midst, but fear has not been cheated. It is embodied in Say Tokyo Kid: fear in the form of his violent political intimidation of the community on behalf of any politician who will pay: and in the form of his own fear of approaching too close to 'things you shouldn't see' (p. 227). The two forms are linked to his anti-visionary stance: the implication is that political violence thrives where people refuse to look into the ultimate secrets of life, including the mystery of death. In his association with a violence that has nothing liberating or creative about it and a fear that intimidates and limits the will to self-liberation, Say Tokyo Kid embodies the fear in people's lives that is the Eshuoro principle.

Professor's death, then, may be understood as the casual destruction of a partly deranged old man by a mindless thug who is afraid of his apparent – but only apparent – power. But it also invites interpretation as something more: as the characteristic antagonism between the Ogun-inspired visionary seeker and the representative of that fear, which intimidates and tries to prevent such seeking. In the pervasive ambivalence of *The Road* the two interpretations are not so much alternatives or distinct 'levels of meaning' as interrelated. Professor's quest may be seen as a delusion that provokes self-destructive retribution; but it may also be understood as the search for an attainment of a revelation that humanizes – or at least potentially humanizes – an erring society. Throughout, and especially at its climax, the play insists that its audience's response inhabit this tension. Professor's final speech is its culminating expression. It can be interpreted as directed at the other characters on stage, or at the audience, or at himself. It speaks of the mirages of the road, 'the sheen [that] raises false forests and a watered haven' (p. 228), the 'ghost lorries' and the shouts and tears that are never heard and are swallowed up in the dust. It speaks of 'dreams' and 'treachery and deceit', the destruction of the 'traveller' at his most confident. But it speaks, above all, of acceptance, of the seeking of an identity between oneself and the way of quest, whatever its dangers and delusions.

The topical political dimension in the form of Say Tokyo Kid's thuggery in the service of corrupt politicians, which has a subdued but significant place in *The Road*, comes to the fore in the tragedies of Soyinka's 'middle-period' drama. The struggles of visionary protagonists, using the resources of traditional wisdom and ritual against oppressive power holders, are now linked very closely to contemporary African political phenomena, specifically the rise of authoritarian leaders such as Kwame Nkrumah and Hastings Banda and the onset of civil war in Soyinka's native country.

In *Kongi's Harvest*, *Madmen and Specialists* and *The Bacchae of Euripides*, written between 1965 and 1973, the lust for power and control is associated with the perversion both of nature and of the forms and ceremonies of traditional ways of using and reverencing natural forces. Kongi insanely and blasphemously wishes to present himself as the very spirit of the harvest; Dr Bero seeks to use his medical knowledge and natural resources, including the herbs collected by his sister under the supervision of the earth mothers, to extend his coercive control of others as a sophisticated scientific torturer. But though Segi and Daodu – combining the best of the traditional and the modernizing – are able to resist Kongi, if not defeat him, and the earth mothers of *Madmen and Specialists* are prepared to destroy the healing products of nature rather than allow them to fall into Dr Bero's hands, it is only when the protagonist is himself a god, Dionysos, that the traditional mode of knowledge and power is utterly triumphant. Even then, it is a deeply ambivalent triumph, for in Soyinka's version of *The Bacchae*, as in Euripides', Dionysos is horrifically brutal in his destruction of the power-crazed Pentheus. Here natural forces, in the form of the Dionysiac frenzy into which the bacchantes and slaves are led by the god, are represented as utterly destroying the repressive (and repressed) authority figure.

Since *Death and the King's Horseman*, which followed *The*

Bacchae of Euripides, Soyinka's writing for the stage has extended the critique of power and its abuses through the satirical comedy of such earlier plays as *The Lion and the Jewel* (1959) and the *Jero* plays (*The Trials of Brother Jero*, 1960; *Jero's Metamorphosis*, 1977), rather than through the tragedy and tragic satire of the drama discussed here. *Opera Wonyosi* (1976) and *A Play of Giants* (1984) are coruscating attacks on the African dictators of the time, the vicious comic-opera 'emperor' of Central Africa, Jean-Bedel Bokassa, Idi Amin of Uganda, Macias Nguemo of Equatorial Guinea, and the military regime of General Yakubu Gowon in Nigeria. *Requiem for a Futurologist* (1983), the agitprop pieces of *Priority Projects* (which toured Nigeria with *Requiem* in 1983) and more recently (and in a much darker mood) *From Zia, with Love* (1992) are sometimes biting exposés of the contemporary Nigerian political and social scene. But it is now a decade and a half since Soyinka last attempted a play in which he seriously explored the roots of the 'lust for power', and the alliance of the spiritual world of African myth and ritual and the rebellious individual quester, who seems to offer the only consistent opposition to it.

Soyinka's achievement is remarkable, rivalled on the African continent only by Athol Fugard in South Africa. In his non-dramatic writings he has explored the terms on which the besieged indigenous culture can assert authentically African values in a modern world dominated by societies that are economically and politically more powerful, and who have long exploited his and other African countries. He has pioneered, with extraordinary imaginative and technical resourcefulness, the creation of dramatic and theatrical forms capable of such an exploration, incorporating and evoking the mythic forces and actual performances of his traditional culture. He has forged ways of juxtaposing different, often contradictory, 'levels' of being and awareness in potently dramatic symbolic locations and actions. He has been fearless in lambasting the abuse and corrupting effects of power, and has not shrunk from naming the names, even at considerable risk to himself. And his importance as a political figure in his own right has had the effect of focusing attention on the central significance of artistic and cultural activity, and theatre in particular, in the struggle and turmoil that Nigeria and other African countries have experienced.

But while no one could seriously question Soyinka's achievement or pre-eminence as an African dramatist, he has in recent years been subjected to critical attack from a younger generation of Nigerian critics. For example, Biodun Jeyifo acknowledges Soyinka's profound and distinctly African humanism, with its concern for and celebration of man's ultimate reconciliation with 'the imponderable verities of his physical and cosmic environment', but suggests that underlying the vision expressed in his drama is 'the reactionary notion that human nature is indivisible or inseparable from nature in general'.[2] Thus a play like *Death and the King's Horseman*, which Jeyifo rightly sees as marking a peak in Soyinka's career in its elaborately tragic expression of the historical rupture in African integration with nature caused by colonialism, can be criticized for its implicit acceptance and rationalization of 'the patriarchal, feudalist code of the ancient Oyo Kingdom',[3] expressed through its portrayal of the tragic hero, Elesin, who embodies the collective will and ethos of his people: a code that in Jeyifo's Marxist perspective is an ideological extension of class rule in the economic and political spheres. What is needed in Africa is not only liberation from neocolonialist domination, but an even more fundamental liberation, from the incapacitating weakness of African productive forces in the face of a still dominating natural environment. Soyinka's play, impressive as it is, can be seen as carrying a dangerously backward-looking ideological 'message'.

Related to this criticism is the charge that, however attractive Soyinka's recreation of Yoruba myth, ritual and metaphysics may be, aesthetically and in other ways, it is a form of what Edward Said calls 'nativism' (see introduction, p. 10). This is ironic, given Soyinka's own critique of negritude and what he has dubbed 'neo-Tarzanism', and the essentialist kinds of thinking informing them. For 'nativism'

---

[2]   Biodun Jeyifo, *The Truthful Lie: Essays in a Sociology of African Drama*, London: New Beacon Books, 1985, p. 60.

[3]   *Ibid.*, p. 34.

is the tendency, characteristic of the post-colonial encounter, to make 'compelling but often demagogic assertions about a native past, history or actuality that seems to stand free not only of the colonizer but of worldly time itself', and thus to 'leave the historical world for the metaphysics of essences ... in a word, to abandon history'.[4] No one could accuse Soyinka of demagogy, but it is certainly arguable that his preoccupation with ritualism, and the myths and metaphysics underlying it, is not ideologically neutral, but carries with it a tendency to abandon history, at least in the last resort, for metaphysical essence.

[4] Edward Said, 'Yeats and Decolonization' in Dennis Walder, ed.,
Literature in the Modern World, Oxford: Oxford University Press,
1990, p. 38.

Athol Fugard and the South African 'workshop' play

While this book was being written far-reaching changes were occurring in the republic of South Africa. After almost half a century during which the racial policies of the government of South Africa gained it a place of special odium in the international community, the system of apartheid has been formally dismantled and in largely trouble-free elections an African National Congress (ANC) government, elected for the first time by a majority of the population, has come to power. The legacy of almost fifty years of apartheid policies will not, of course, be easily overcome. Since the accession of the Nationalist Party in 1948, the state in South Africa has systematically used its powers – physical, political and economic – to dominate and coerce the majority non-white population in the name of so-called 'separate development'. The result is a degree of social injustice extraordinary by any standards, and communities torn by very high rates of crime, political violence and a multitude of other ills. Though the current mood is justifiably optimistic and hopeful, Nelson Mandela's government faces enormous challenges. A black population mostly living in squalid conditions in the townships and 'homelands' has large expectations of rapid improvement in their standards of living and quality of life. Many of the white minority are nervous about the threat to their way of life, and some, especially amongst the Afrikaans-speaking Boers, are unwilling to give up the substance of apartheid, even if they have no choice but to accept the formal changes. And as the black-on-black violence between ANC and Inkatha supporters before the elections clearly demonstrated, there is a terrifying potential for large-scale factional and ethnic violence in the new republic.

The momentous political changes now in progress have large cultural implications and entail a new artistic agenda. In spite of censorship and repression a substantial body of literature and theatre, which is essentially a documenting of and protest against apartheid, has developed, some of it of great distinction. But in the new circumstances, with the establishment of majority rule, the emphasis is bound to change, presumably primarily to the role of the arts and culture in the forging of a unitary, multiracial state to which the ANC has always been committed. Foreshadowing the need for such a change, the veteran ANC activist Albie Sachs evoked the vision of a future South African culture in which 'the grandchildren of white immigrants can join in the *toyi toyi* – even if slightly out of step – or recite the poems of Wally Serote, just as the grandchildren of Dinizulu can read with pride the writings of Olive Schreiner'.[1] To do so, of course, will involve breaking down formidable barriers of suspicion and ignorance; and it is hard to see how such a radical cultural 'revolution' can occur without fundamental economic and social changes, which are themselves more likely to reinforce than to diminish racial and class antagonism.

It will be fascinating to observe the directions in which South African theatre will go in the next few years. One possible direction is in the further development of a genre that has in fact been a distinctive product of the old apartheid system, but which in seeking to protest against and transcend it has opened up theatrical possibilities that may well be a major source of creativity in the future. This is the 'workshop' drama in the making of which black and white artists have collaborated, in the past to challenge the very basis of apartheid. As Anne Fuchs points out, some of the companies that have engaged in this kind of work can be seen as 'trying to live and create a non-racial society through their very association, with blacks and whites contributing specific cultural artefacts and techniques which were synthesised into a new form of theatre', which was itself 'a metonymic image of a New South Africa'.[2]

[1] Albie Sachs, 'When Art Takes Liberties', *The Independent*, London, 18 April 1990, p. 13.
[2] Anne Fuchs, 'The New South African Theatre: Beyond Fugard' in Bruce King, ed., *Post-Colonial English Drama* , p. 174.

The range of collaboration that has taken place in South African theatre as a response to the reality of apartheid is wide and varied, going well beyond the specific genre of the 'workshop' play. It includes theatre originated by blacks and intended primarily for black audiences that, sometimes of necessity, has made use of white directors, devisers and managements. Examples embrace black writers such as Fatima Dike (*The Sacrifice of Kreli*) and Zakes Mda (*The Hill*), whose work has been directed by the white director Rob Amato at white venues such as The Space in Cape Town; companies of black (or predominantly black) actors such as the Serpent Players, Workshop '71, Mirror One, and agitprop workers' theatre groups that have benefited from the artistic and organizational skills of white activists such as Athol Fugard, Barney Simon and Robert McLaren (Mshengu); and even – paradoxically, given their political principles and aims – the post-1976 Soweto Uprising Black Consciousness groups such as those associated with Matsemela Manaka and Maishe Maponya, which have sometimes enjoyed relatively little success with township audiences (unlike the largely apolitical, some might say reactionary, drama of the most popular township playwright, Gibson Kente) and have had to accept white patronage both at home (notably at the Market Theatre in Johannesburg) and on tours abroad. It also embraces white writers, most famously Fugard, whose plays have either required black actors or have been devised with the collaboration of black actors.

From this diversity of co-operation has come a wide range of dramatic products to consider alongside, on the one hand, the non-collaborative theatre of African township playwrights such as Gibson Kente and, on the other, the all-white theatre imported from the West or created with it as the model. But a central preoccupation – the desire and search for an assured self-identity – is often discernible in this drama, though it has found expression in a wide variety of forms, both theatrically and ideologically. For example, in plays written and produced under the inspiration of the Black Consciousness Movement (BCM) the quest for identity is often explicitly polemical in tone, seeking to politicize its non-white audiences about the nature of their oppression and to delineate and reinforce effective resistance to it. Ideologically very different from the products of the BCM, but nevertheless a play centrally engaged with the issue of black identity, is *uNosilimela* (1973), Credo Mutwa's collaboration with the Marxist white director and producer Robert McLaren (Mshengu). *uNosilimela* is a fantastical, 'return to roots' epic with a bewildering array of characters, earthly and supernatural, combining mythic and contemporary time. Its 'message' is that to regain their authentic identity, their original purity of being, black South Africans must shun the cities with their imported cultures and religions and return to their material and cultural roots on the land.

Yet another example – and one which brings us to the genre that interests us especially in this discussion – is *Woza Albert!* (1981), the product of a collaboration between the veteran Market Theatre director Barney Simon and two former actors with Gibson Kente's company, Percy Mtwa and Mbongeni Ngema. Here, the religious idea of identity as spiritual members of one body, Christ, constitutes the central conceit, which is an exploration of what might happen if Christ, making his Second Coming, were to choose the republic of South Africa and arrive at Jan Smuts airport in a jumbo jet. In a fast-moving series of comic scenes offering a panorama of black South African life, *Woza Albert!* exposes the real effects of apartheid policies, which the government has always hypocritically claimed to be sanctioned by its Christian Nationalist principles. In its moving finale, it adapts the Christian notion of resurrection to summon up the spirits of the dead heroes and heroines, black and white, of the liberation struggle in South Africa. Here, the audience – black and white – is offered an image of solidarity, an ideal transcending social and ethnic difference in a revolutionary identity based on struggle and its illustrious history of martyrs.

Woza Albert! was devised from an original idea by Mtwa and Ngema with the aid of the dramaturgical skills of Barney Simon, and it represents one of the most artistically and commercially successful examples of a by now well-established tradition of making theatre through 'workshops' involving the contributions of (usually) black actors and (usually) white director – writers. This and other examples of collaboration between white and non-white theatre practitioners have not only been responses to apartheid but also, inevitably and in more than one sense, products of it.

Take for example the plays developed by Athol Fugard, John Kani and Winston Ntshona, which pioneered the tradition of black–white workshop collaborations. *Sizwe Bansi is Dead* and *The Island* – which will be discussed in more detail shortly – are powerful indictments of, and protests against, apartheid, performances of which in many countries helped to educate audiences about the true nature and effects of the policies of the South African regime. To achieve them, Fugard and his performers had to conduct their artistic collaboration in defiance of cultural 'separate development', given legal substance in the entertainment segregation laws that prohibited or severely restricted multiracial theatrical activity. (Racial segregation of audiences was introduced in 1961.) At the same time, in a society under apartheid such as South Africa's, even an artist like Fugard, who has been utterly hostile to the system and from very early on in his career had close social and professional contacts with blacks, was bound as a white to be ignorant about aspects of black experience and could not adequately explore important features of his own society without the substantial creative contributions of black collaborators.

Ironically, then, apartheid has encouraged innovative ways of creating for the stage and of using the dramatic medium – most notably the 'workshop' play – that transcend the usual theatrical division of labour. In much of this work, the actors become 'writers', as much the 'authors' of their script as its performers; and the playwright becomes a combination of creative *agent provocateur*, director, dramaturg and script editor. If Fugard's resources as a thinker, writer and director were indispensable to the making of plays about black South African experience during the 1960s and seventies, so also were both the acting skills and the life experiences of John Kani and Winston Ntshona. Such collaborations, pursued in the face of apartheid ideology and legality, have not been without their tensions. As John Kani made clear in a BBC radio interview, his readiness to work with Fugard required his overcoming of personal suspicion based on his initial reaction to a man of a race he hated. And it may be that Africans who have worked with a white director – dramaturg who has enjoyed considerably greater power in the creative and production process have had reservations about the nature of the final product, however successful in many respects the collaboration has been.

From what has already been said, it is evident that it would be a gross error to equate artistically serious and innovative South African theatre exclusively with the work of Athol Fugard and his collaborators. But it is nonetheless true that Fugard has been not only the best known but also quite simply the best dramatist to have emerged from, and made plays about, that troubled country. His long career in South African theatre – as an actor and director as well as a dramatist – embraces a remarkable variety of forms of collaboration that have always been artistically fruitful. Even in his earliest work Fugard experimented with improvisational methods, having his black actors play a creative role in the devising of the script. In *Sizwe Bansi is Dead* (1972) and *The Island* (1973) he helped pioneer the distinctively South African genre of the 'workshop' play. And in single authorship plays such as *Blood Knot* (1961), *Boesman and Lena* (1969), *Statements after an Arrest under the Immorality Act* (1974) and *'Master Harold' ... and the Boys* (1982) Fugard has witnessed and chronicled the effects of apartheid on black and white alike. Taken as a whole – though of course an as yet unfinished whole – Fugard's work can be seen as a kind of collaboration at another level, whatever the particular contexts in which specific plays were made. This collaboration is between two distinguishable but in reality always interweaving impulses: Fugard's commitment to an existentialist vision of identity and behaviour, influenced initially by his reading of Camus; and his equally strong commitment to witness and record in his theatre the oppressive operation and effects of the social and political system of apartheid.

In this pervasive sense the particular conditions of apartheid have been crucial not only in generating new forms of collaboration, and hence new methods of working and new dramatic genres in South African theatre, but also in encouraging, at least in the drama of its major playwright, a particularly rich perspective in which to explore social being and interaction. To make matters more concrete it is worth turning to Fugard's *Notebooks*, the creative diary that he kept through much of the 1960s and seventies, where he describes a workshop session with Kani and Ntshona, the methods of which were shortly to be developed in the creation of *Sizwe Bansi.*

The two actors played waiters serving a lounge full of arrogant whites in a local hotel. Using only a table and empty chair, Fugard asked them to wait on what was evidently a symbol of 'whiteness'. He then invited them to analyze what he calls their 'sub-text experiences' in their relationships to the table and chair, which he describes as evoking a complicated range of feelings, including resentment, subordination and dependence. Fugard rather cryptically notes the questions that Kani, in particular, was provoked into asking by this kind of work: '– who am I? Where am I? Who is where? The mask and the face behind the mask. The ontological dilemma arising out of "role" playing' (p. 202). Whatever the precise nature of this 'dilemma' might be, it is clear enough that the method used in such workshops was intended to provoke the actors into exploring the furthest accessible recesses of their own psyches and bringing what they found there into their performances. And in this case the psychic material had to do with the central, dominant relationship of their society – that of white master and black servant.

The self as the play of masks; society as a 'theatre' in which 'actors' perform their 'roles'; being as the dialectic of self and other: these are notions that Fugard, with his debt to Camus and others, has imbued with a particular existentialist emphasis, but which the theatre, to which they have a special appropriateness, has in any case long been exploring. Yet in the context of the last half century of South African history such preoccupations cannot be divorced from the realities of apartheid. For by its very nature that system has denied, in the name of 'separate development', the common humanity which must be the basis of that open-ended potential for mutual expressiveness which constitutes social 'theatricality'. So the 'scenarios' and 'roles' possible in the theatre of everyday life under apartheid have been extremely limited. In general they have not escaped externally 'overdetermined' forms of interaction and the modes of expressiveness associated with them. The white 'madam' and her black maid interact daily, but the faces – or masks – that they present to each other are narrowly determined by prevailing notions of what is considered acceptable in the white mistress–black maid relationship. Similarly, the possibilities of expressiveness between white and black men at work are strictly limited, in such a system, by the boss–'boy' relationship that structures the scenarios, roles and dialogue generally considered acceptable for them to engage in. But as Fanon and others have shown, the relative 'poverty' of these inter-actions, dominated by external forces and racial stereotypes, does not mean that there is a corresponding poverty of response behind the masks. On the contrary, the rigidity of self-presentation *vis-à-vis* the 'other' in such a system conceals turbulent depths of affect, in which desire, dependence and hatred of the self as well as of the other are swirling currents.

So the conditions of apartheid have led not only to innovation in form and the methods of devising drama, but at the same time to an exploration of the conditions of its social reality – in much of this work, the nature of its particular forms of 'social theatricality'. As Fugard's description of his workshop with Kani and Ntshona suggests, their collaboration was concerned not only with documenting – 'witnessing' in Fugard's phrase – the conditions of black life in South Africa, but also with exploring the effects on blacks (and, to some extent, whites also) of the rigorous curtailment of the potential for social expressiveness between the races, and the appropriate response to this.

> John was scheduled to do 20 minutes of newspaper improvisation before the play proper started. He went out visibly nervous. An hour-and-a-half later he was still there, the audience in the palm of his hand. (Fugard, quoted in Stephen Gray, ed., *Athol Fugard*)

Apart from being a salutary reminder of how far a particular performance may differ from the printed text, Fugard's reminiscence of Kani's acting in *Sizwe Bansi* testifies to one of the main reasons for its international success – the extraordinary degree of audience empathy the original production was able to achieve, even in audiences largely ignorant of South African realities. Much of this, no doubt, has to do with Kani's remarkable skills as an actor, his capacity for bringing energy, commitment and personal truth to the stage. But it may also have to do with experiencing, in Kani's or another's successful performance, the realization that theatre is most powerful in its statements when it is most itself, brimming over with its own distinctive inventiveness.

For we can imagine Kani, in those opening minutes of the play, peopling the stage with an array of characters and incidents, the texture of a whole society, all refracted through the compelling fictional personality of Styles the photographer; and yet all of this must be conjured up from almost nothing, merely from the physical resources of the actor John Kani. Through such a virtuoso performance as Kani's we are not only informed about the detailed reality of black life in South Africa, we also witness the mastering of it, the process by which it is brought to consciousness, shaped by means of the theatrical imagination and the power of the actor in performance celebrated.

As Styles, Kani played a character who in his role of township photographer understands himself as the witness of his people's lives, the recorder of their dreams, the mediator of their experiences to the audience. And in his opening monologue Styles role-plays a succession of characters: himself previously as a worker in the Ford plant, at home with his family and as photographer; as 'Baas' Bradley; as the man who's just got standard six; as members of the large family who come in for a group portrait; and so on. Styles's monologue and the role-playing that goes on in it serve several functions, such as creating a context for the action that is to follow and bringing the audience into the play through humour and inventiveness. They do something else: they make a vivid theatrical reality of a fundamental contradiction in South African society with which the entire play is concerned. For here we have a black actor playing with great skill a black character who is remarkably protean and versatile in the range of characters and events he can image for the audience. Here is South African experience presented from a black viewpoint in a way that invigoratingly displays – through the acting of Kani, the created character of Styles and the exuberant theatricalism of that opening monologue – the strength and versatility of the black cultural 'personality'. And yet the point of the story of Styles's life at the Ford factory – and specifically the visit by Mr Ford – is that for whites, blacks simply do not exist as 'real' people. The theatrical experience, based on the actor's personal experience and the dramatic structuring of it through improvisation, contradicts the 'message' of white ideology identified by the play.

When he first enters the photographic studio Sizwe/Robert is the opposite of Styles, so diffident and inept a role-player that he doesn't know how to go about using theatrical expressiveness to image his 'dream' for his wife Nowetu back in King William's Town. But with a little encouragement and direction he is soon able to create two roles for himself, which Styles then records on film: as chief messenger at Feltex, sitting in his office with a map of the world behind him; and as a 'man about town' striding through the City of the Future. The episode is quite short, but in the course of it Sizwe/ Robert develops from someone who hardly seems to know his own name to a man who, as social 'actor' in Styles's theatrical 'strong-room of dreams', has at least established the images of self he wishes to project. He has made the first steps towards an expressive versatility that Styles has already brilliantly exemplified.

As the play demonstrates its own theatrical versatility, using deft narrative transitions to change story and viewpoint, we witness the process by which Sizwe Bansi becomes Robert Zwelinzima. But this is not an easy transition, of the kind that we have witnessed Styles so effortlessly displaying in his earlier role-playing. On the contrary, Sizwe finds it well-nigh impossible to even consider 'dying' as himself and adopting the name of the dead man in the alley outside Sky's place. This is not surprising, since it is evidently a transformation, an act of social 'theatricality', of an altogether different order from those we have so far witnessed. To forsake one's own name and take on another man's identity; that is the ultimate act of versatility required of the social 'actor'. The idea of transferring the photograph from Sizwe's invalid passbook into the dead man's valid one, and vice versa, is of course Buntu's, and it is he who articulates the central statement of the play as he struggles to persuade Sizwe to accept his plan. To Sizwe's objection that he cannot live as another man's ghost Buntu argues that he is already a ghost:

When the white man looked at you at the Labour Bureau what did he see? A man with dignity or a bloody passbook with an NI number? Isn't that a ghost? When the white man sees you walk down the street and calls out, 'Hey, John! Come here' ... to you, Sizwe Bansi ... isn't that a ghost? Or when his little child calls you 'Boy' ... you a man, circumcised with a wife and four children ... isn't that a ghost? Stop fooling yourself. All I'm saying is be a real ghost, if that is what they want, what they've turned us into. Spook them into hell, man! (p. 38)

This is the play's statement of the fundamental condition of social theatricality, the terms on which people may be expressive to each other, in apartheid society. A name, argues Buntu, is of no importance, indeed merely the source of false pride, in a society where white men regard blacks as entirely interchangeable.

Horrified though Sizwe/Robert is by Buntu's argument, the text presents its formulation as coinciding with what, in performance, is perhaps the play's most moving moment. Disgusted and despairing at his new friend's readiness to walk away from the dead body, Sizwe asks if Buntu would do the same if he were the corpse: 'Would you leave me lying there, wet with your piss? I wish I was dead. I wish I was dead because I don't care a damn about anything any more' (p. 34). And with these words he turns to the audience and tears off his clothes, asserting through his words and actions his essential, common humanity. Though it only does so ironically, Sizwe/Robert's symbolic gesture sanctions Buntu's strategy, which relies on a different interpretation of Sizwe's assertion that we share a fundamental humanity. If this is so, why not assume the identity of another if that is what is required to survive?

Buntu resorts to role-play to reinforce the effect his words have had on Sizwe/Robert. The new Robert in the line on pay-day at Feltex; the new Robert walking into Sales House to buy a suit; the new Robert becoming a respected member of his local church. These are the possible benefits that role-play brings home to the reluctant 'actor'. But for these desirable things to come about Sizwe must learn his lines – or in this case his NI number. The rehearsal is successful; Sizwe learns his number and assumes his new name. The play ends with the optimistic image of the man once named Sizwe Bansi back in Styles's studio striding through the City of the Future as Mr Robert Zwelinzima, man about town.

Theatre here is not merely witnessing the reality of black lives and oppression under apartheid, it is investigating the condition of social theatricality itself within that system. From Styles's opening monologue right to the end of the play, *Sizwe Bansi* demonstrates the imperative for the black person in South Africa to be an 'actor', to present an enforcedly 'acceptable' mask to his or her white masters. The play becomes a dramatized argument about the terms on which such 'acting' is acceptable to blacks; and it argues for the exploitation of such theatricality, in spite of natural inhibitions, to survive and perhaps even prosper. It is not only a play conceived as a weapon of political struggle: it promotes the statement that 'acting' – the power to be knowingly protean in appearance, to use the expressive qualities associated with theatrical performance – can and should be a weapon of struggle. Or as Fugard had written in his notebook a decade or so earlier: 'Revolt (meaning) can only come with consciousness ... Without consciousness we become victims instead of actors – even if it is still only a question of acting victims. And in this make-believe of our lives the audience is self.'[3]

Sizwe Bansi assumes a new identity to survive, in an act which Buntu articulates as a kind of rebellion – 'spooking the whites'. In their next workshop production, *The Island*, Fugard, Kani and Ntshona again presented not only theatre but theatricality as an affirmative value in the struggle against apartheid. The denial of personal identity to blacks by whites within that system is now dramatized in its most extreme and painful expression – imprisonment on Robben Island, where rebels are sent 'to be lost between life and death'. The focus is on what, in its most cruel form, the regime can do to one's identity, ultimately even annihilating the very sense of selfhood. Theatricality – here in the form of a play within the play, the rehearsals and performance of John's and Winston's improvised

---

[3] Mary Benson, ed., *Notebooks 1960/1977*, London: Faber & Faber, 1983, p. 107.

version of *Antigone* at a prison concert – is the means by which the prisoners make their statement of resistance.

'Look, Winston, try to understand, man, ... this is Theatre.' Winston's difficulties with theatre include learning the plot of *Antigone* and doing something that he is tempted to believe is merely child's play. Most of all, he hates being laughed at by John when he first puts on his character's wig and false breasts, which exacerbates the basic problem – that he does not want to play a woman. John makes the point that the audience, though it will laugh because it knows it is Winston behind all this 'rubbish', will not always do so: 'There'll come a time when they'll stop laughing, and that will be the time when our Antigone hits them with her words' (p. 61). The final scene of *The Island* validates John's insight, demonstrating how theatre can overcome even the most grotesque inadequacies to 'hit' us with the truths it speaks. But the performance of *Antigone* constitutes even more than a statement of ethical truths by men to whom the fable peculiarly applies. It is the means by which Winston, who has been so recalcitrant about the performance, honours his personal commitment to the cause that has brought him here even though his own personality may eventually be effaced by its rigours. Theatricality cannot do for Winston what it may, if he is lucky, do for Sizwe/Robert. It cannot give him an identity with which, in his modest way, he can resist apartheid and perhaps even prosper. But the willing loss of personal identity to become temporarily another, in this case a dramatic fiction, does allow Winston to make his statement, even if one day he will eventually suffer the permanent extinction of his selfhood when he becomes like old Harry, who has forgotten himself, his personality turned to the stone he so perfectly fashions.

In these two *Statements* plays the collaboration between Fugard, Kani and Ntshona permits the white playwright to explore existentialist themes centrally related to the black experience of apartheid as an oppressive system, and the black actors to explore and in a sense master their experience of that system, through the resources of performance itself. Deeply imbedded in the conditions and dilemmas of racial oppression in South Africa, their collaboration 'opens up' the problem, for blacks, of identity and role in that society, faced as they have been by the enforced dichotomy between mask and face, between what is there and what can be shown. The pioneering work that the dramatist and his black collaborators did on these 'workshop' plays came as a fertile departure for Fugard, breaking a creative 'block' that he experienced after writing *Boesman and Lena*. In this and other earlier single authorship plays such as *Blood Knot*, Fugard had explored how consciousness and self-identity are constructed in basically 'theatrical' ways in the context of black life under apartheid. But for all their dramatic interest and power these earlier plays are vulnerable to the criticism that their existentialist themes are not adequately matched by their white author's capacity to document realistically the actual experience of life under apartheid for non-whites. And since 1975, when Fugard turned away from the collaborative work with black actors that flowered in *Sizwe Bansi is Dead* and *The Island*, it is noticeable that most of his dramatic writing has been concerned with exclusively or primarily white South African experience, or, as in *Dimetos* (1975), with autobiographical experience abstracted from the immediate circumstances of apartheid South Africa. (Exceptions are his best post-*Statements* play, *'Master Harold'* ... *and the Boys* and his most recent plays, *My Children! My Africa!* (1989) and *Playland* (1992).)

The collaborative 'workshop' plays, then, represent an especially fruitful experiment in Fugard's career, and his decision not to explore further that method and genre arguably entailed a loss not entirely compensated by the undeniable achievements of his subsequent writing. If Fugard renounced the possibilities of the genre, others, however, did not. Indeed, in other hands it has continued to develop, to become one of the most distinctive and exciting genres that South African theatrical expression has developed in response to the apartheid system. Mention has already been made of a particularly successful example of the 'workshop' play, both artistically and commercially, in *Woza Albert!* When Percy Mtwa and Mbongeni Ngema turned to Barney Simon for help in developing their idea for a play, they did so in the knowledge that Simon was already the veteran of a series of workshop productions involving multiracial casts. Over the years Simon's collaborative workshop experiments at the Market

Theatre have produced such pieces as *Cincinatti, Call Me Woman, Black Dog, Born in the RSA* and *Starbrites*. As well as its own productions, the Market has also fulfilled an important function by hosting multiracial and African companies and giving them the opportunity to develop and present their work, sometimes when it might otherwise have been impossible, or at least extremely difficult, to do so. A company that has enjoyed the Market's hospitality and which is a particularly interesting example of black–white collaboration is Junction Avenue. This began as a white student group and developed, with the addition of black actors from the by now defunct Workshop '71, into a multiracial troupe under a white director, Malcolm Purkey. Junction's workshopped productions include *The Fantastical History of a Useless Man, Randlords and Rotgut, Marabi, Tooth and Nail*, and its internationally successful production of the mid-1980s, *Sophiatown*, which powerfully combined Western and African performance styles into a play questioning whether black and white could successfully coexist in South Africa.

The new political situation creates a profound challenge for theatre practitioners of all races who wish to give truthful and insightful expression on stage to current South African realities. Fugard himself, in an interview on BBC Radio 3 before transmission of his latest work, *Playland*, has spoken of the completely new situation that has come about with the ending of apartheid. In the past, he points out, the moral dilemma was clear-cut because the issues themselves were so unambiguous; the choice was stark, for the artist as for other individuals – to say 'yes' or 'no' to apartheid. Now, the moral dilemmas are becoming much more complex, much more a matter of recognizing and negotiating a terrain of grey areas rather than confronting a landscape of blacks and whites. And Fugard sees *Playland*, with its themes of understanding and coming to terms with the past, its concern with repentance and forgiveness, as the beginning of his personal response to the new circumstances and the new challenges. He is bound to continue and develop his lengthy collaboration with black actors, especially John Kani; and it will be interesting to see whether what he has described as the 'rebirth of Fugard the writer' includes a return to some form of the work inaugurated by *Sizwe Bansi is Dead* and *The Island*. Whether it does or not, it seems likely that the racially collaborative 'workshop' play will continue beyond its origins, as a distinctive response to apartheid domination, to become a rich theatrical seam to be tapped in the new South Africa.

Badal Sircar's Third Theatre of Calcutta

Calcutta, along with Bombay, Madras and Delhi, was among the major urban centres of British colonial rule in India. The dominance of Calcutta sprang largely from its historical location as the commercial heart of the East India Company, following the British victory at the Battle of Plassey and Robert Clive's acquisition of the management of Bengal revenues in 1765. Many Europeans made immense fortunes from the trade privileges and land revenues exacted via a hierarchical system of landlords or *zamindars* in the profitable districts of Bihar and Bengal. Calcutta was to continue as the seat of British imperial rule of India, home of governor-generals and viceroys, from 1773 until 1911 when, following the coronation of the king-emperor George V, the capital was transferred to Delhi.

Unsurprisingly, the colonialists brought with them their own cultural traditions and practices, at such time as relative peace, and unquestionable prosperity, allowed these luxuries. The first theatre, called simply the Calcutta Theatre, was built during the period of Warren Hastings's governor-generalship in 1779, and ran for more than three decades until an accumulation of debts forced its closure. In every way the numerous theatres that followed over the next 100 years were modelled on the then contemporary practices of English,

* Plays in English translation referred to in this chapter are as follows: *Evam Indrajit*, reprinted in *Three Modern Indian Plays*, Oxford University Press, New Delhi, 1989; *Shesh Nei (There's No End)* in *Enact*, 59, New Delhi, 1971; *Three Plays: Procession, Bhoma, Stale News*, Seagull Books, Calcutta, 1985; *Beyond the Land of Hattamala* in *Beyond the Land of Hattamala and Scandal in Fairyland*, Seagull Books, Calcutta, 1992.

specifically London, theatres. In spite, therefore, of the oppressive heat and humidity, audiences, conventionally attired, would gather in indoor venues, architecturally designed in congruence with the Drury Lane and Covent Garden theatres of the day, even if not quite as ambitiously scaled and ornamented.

The dramatic fare on offer was, similarly, drawn from that available to play-goers at home. Visiting actors from the mother country were naturally extremely popular. While it was consistent with assimilatory colonial cultural ambitions to allow a rising English-educated *bhadralog* class to *attend* performances, doubtless for purposes of self-improvement, the appearance on the stage in 1848 of a 'Native Gentleman', Baishnav Charan Auddy, as reported in a letter to the *Calcutta Star*, apparently set 'the whole world of Calcutta agog' with his debut performance in Shakespeare's tragedy as 'a real unpainted nigger Othello'.[1]

The first public proscenium stage, in imitation of British theatrical tradition yet specifically dedicated for the performance of plays by and for Bengalis, was provocatively called the National Theatre and opened in 1872 with a play that had aroused considerable controversy in its earlier productions. Dinabandhu's play *Nildurpan* has been regarded as the first Bengali 'political protest' play. Its narrative deals with the exploitation of a landowner's family and peasant farmers by British indigo planters. Consistent with the melodramatic impulses of the conventional colonial theatre of its time, one scene features a peasant's daughter narrowly saved from imminent rape by an indigo planter, one Mr Rogue. The dramatic portrayal of such behaviour by a white male, in spite of accurately according with the observations of exploitation by the indigenous population (and perhaps by some of the more enlightened colonialist themselves), seems to have been initially vigorously opposed and gradually grudgingly tolerated by the Europeans. Especially irksome must have been the memory of the unfortunate Reverend Long, a missionary who had received a one-month gaol term for translating the play shortly after its composition in 1860.

---

[1] Kironmoy Raha, *Bengali Theatre*, New Delhi: National Book Trust, 1978, p. 10.

At any rate, barely a dozen years later it was doing excellent business at the box-office.

While these examples may indicate the dominance of colonial theatre in shaping the practice, if not always the ideology, of a developing Bengali theatre, it is important not to overlook the parallel presence of a long-established indigenous folk theatre tradition specific to the region. *Jatra*, though generally viewed with contempt by the bhadralog urban elite of Calcutta during the colonial period (and by its intelligentsia for different reasons at various times since), enjoyed, and in greatly modified form continues to enjoy, considerable popularity. It is not difficult to imagine why English-educated Bengalis rejected their homegrown theatre in favour of a colonial import, given the inevitable pressure to conform within a dominant cultural and social milieu.

Jatra, which means 'to go in a procession', has evolved through several centuries, and its origins are certainly devotional. There is no single interpretation of its genesis, though one common one is that it grew out of the musical enactment of episodes from the life of the Hindu god Krishna. The briefest of outlines will establish its main features, concentrating on the physical aspects of the performance space and style of presentation.

Though traditionally played on the ground, jatra is now performed on a square, platform stage (asar) of sixteen feet in length and breadth and two and a half feet high. There is no scenery as such, with the exception of a chair, which may have all kinds of symbolic possibilities. Other properties may be brought on to the stage by the actors. A narrow passage of some sixty feet, marked with bamboo sticks and rope, leads off to a 'green room' from one corner of the stage. Performers make all their entrances and exits along this corridor, which may also serve as an acting area, such as a road or pathway. Playing conventions allow the performer either to 'de-role' once off the main acting area, or continue in character along the gangway. The audience is seated on all four sides of the playing space, customarily with women on one side and men on the other three.

The playing style of jatra has largely been determined by the fact that it takes place in the open air in front of a large audience. As one might expect, this has created a forceful, demonstrative, vocally and physically powerful style. This is anything but naturalistic in approach.

One of the most interesting characters of jatra is the Vivek, which means 'conscience'. The Vivek developed essentially in the twentieth century and his function is succinctly summarized by Balwant Gargi:

> When a character does something wrong, the Vivek turns up to warn him in song. If a king is doing an injustice, the Vivek suddenly appears to check him. Dressed like a madman – his eyes glazed, his head and feet bare, his beard tangled – he wears a robe of black, saffron, or white. His movements are sharp and conclusive. He enters the gangway on the run and disappears in the same way. The Vivek has a definite dramatic function. He comments on the action by his song, externalizes the feeling of the character, plays his double and puts questions to him. He is everybody's shadow, a running commentary on actions and events. He lives in the past, present, and future. [2]

Before the advent of microphones and amplification it was necessary for the actors to project their voices out into the crowd, in all directions, turning in presentational style to face the four sides of watching spectators. Musicians, seated at opposite edges of the acting square, provide the accompaniment to the half a dozen songs that are now performed during a four-hour production. Originally, performances lasted much longer, beginning in the afternoon and continuing until dawn, including some sixty or more songs.

Other changes have greatly affected the development of jatra over time. In the nineteenth century a gradual secularization of the plays' themes took place, moving away from the religious stories of Krishna, Rama, Siva and Kali to historical and romantic stories. Improvised prose dialogue began to supplement the music and songs. Originally female characters would have been played by male actors, though women have routinely performed in jatra troupes for many years now. In fact jatra was to become criticized for its over-salacious

---

[2] Balwant Gargi, *Folk Theatre of India*, Calcutta: Rupa & Co., 1991, p. 29.

emphasis on erotic encounters, songs and dances. To compete with the developing film industry, an emphasis was laid on intricacy of plot, murders, love scenes, and a fast-moving pace to keep the audience's attention. Jatra's content became viewed as largely reactionary by those for whom the political and social content of drama was paramount.

However, the performance forms and styles of jatra were not always seen as incompatible with 'serious drama'. Towards the end of the Second World War, in 1943, the political theatre movement in India was founded with the establishment of the Indian People's Theatre Association (IPTA). This organization arose from the Communist Party of India and embraced writers, musicians, actors and other intellectuals under a broadly anti-fascist, anti-imperialist, Marxist banner. The alliance was eventually to disintegrate through factionalism, but interestingly the models of theatre practice to which the predominantly middle-class members of the IPTA first turned were precisely the folk traditions such as jatra, of which they had scant firsthand experience. The appalling famine of Bengal, between 1943 and 1944 when several million peasants died, was to provide powerful motivation for those early productions even if 'folk' elements were barely discernible in the performances.[3]

Utpal Dutt, a key figure in post-colonial Bengali political theatre, was involved with the IPTA until 1951. Subsequently, his People's Little Theatre did perhaps more than any other to politicize jatra in performances of Dutt's own plays, drawing on topical social issues, satirizing contemporary political figures, rousing audiences of thousands with tub-thumping Marxist rhetoric, with Dutt himself employing the folk form's melodramatic and operatic acting traditions to maximum effect, invariably in the role of menacing villain. Rustom Bharucha explains that since independence, jatra has thrived in rural areas, where villagers were to become 'quite accustomed to seeing Marx, Lenin, and Mao appear in the coveted roles of the heroes'.

It is against this background that Badal Sircar's work must be

---

[3] See Rustom Bharucha, *Rehearsals of Revolution, The Political Theater of Bengal*, Calcutta: Seagull Books, 1983, pp. 40–1.

considered. In many ways Sircar embodies the contradictions of his generation. Born in Calcutta in 1925, his parents were Christian, his father being for many years Professor of the Scottish Church School. It was, therefore, a pre-independence, British-style educational system, with instruction in English, that he negotiated. For so many of his generation, the lowering of the Union Flag in 1947 marked a year of enormous potential for change. Now, nearly fifty years on, the practical political solutions that have been offered by the local Marxist government after many years in office, to address the myriad problems of the region, are under close scrutiny, as allegations of corruption and betrayal contribute to the disillusionment of left-leaning intellectuals and a widespread popular cynicism with the political process.

In his writing Sircar is not explicitly politically partisan, insofar as he refuses to align himself with any one political party, preferring instead to preserve the integrity that this independence has afforded him. His motivation for writing has, however, become characterized by a passionate personal response to the injustices and oppressions endured in the lives of the poor and disenfranchised, both of his own country and beyond. The themes of his plays are located in struggle; against the inertia of complacency and ignorance. Yet his plays do not have the revolutionary rhetoric of his contemporary Dutt. They seem to depend instead on a recognition that responsibility for change must rest at an individual level before a collective response is possible.

Sircar has written, and continues to write, in Bengali. One of the central paradoxes created by British colonialism in India has been its legacy of a common though not unifying language. As a proposed national language, Hindi has failed to develop deep enough roots across the subcontinent, both in the south, where the imposition of many a northern dictate has been resisted, and certainly in Bengal where cultural identity is equally firmly anchored in language, oral and written. For Westerners, the primacy of Bengali as a language capable of supreme poetic evocation and lyricism was confirmed, if such confirmation were needed, with Rabindranath Tagore's Nobel prize for literature in 1913. However today, when groups of middle-class Indians come together from across the subcontinent, bringing with them mother tongues of Hindi, Urdu, Bengali, Tamil, Telegu, Malayalam, Kannada and others, it seems ironic that often the common language is one associated with an era of British colonialism in India that ended almost half a century ago. Although Badal Sircar's education has brought him an assured and fluent command of English, his view is that it would be an entirely inappropriate language for the theatre to which he is committed to write.

Badal Sircar's work has changed considerably over the thirty years or so since he became recognized as a potent force in contemporary Indian theatre. While he has remained a 'metropolitan' writer, in the sense that he has always had Calcutta as his home base, both the themes and the forms (in spite of his avowed uninterest in the latter) of his theatre have developed in non-traditional ways. 'Tradition' is clearly a notion that requires careful examination in light of the context within which Sircar's work must necessarily be placed. As should be clear by now, the notion of a *single* theatrical tradition in respect of contemporary Bengali theatre needs to be rejected in favour of an acknowledgement of the twin and often intertwining roots of theatrical practice, reaching back more than 200 years, that embrace both the 'traditional' (Western) proscenium arch *and* outdoor folk theatre 'traditions'. In fact Sircar's 'Third Theatre', as he has named it, synthesizes elements from each.

The transition in Sircar's writing, following perhaps his best known play *Evam Indrajit* (1962), was stimulated by his desire to move away from the confines of the proscenium arch stage towards the discovery of other kinds of performance spaces, and a concomitant emphasis on the fundamental importance of a direct relationship between performer and spectator. It is possible to trace this change in approach to the physical structure of the performance place via both Western and Bengali lineages. In *The Third Theatre*, Sircar's book based on a project that aimed to examine a theatre which might act as a rural/urban link, he writes:

> And still, the Indian city theatre almost unquestioningly
> accepts the proscenium theatre imported from a Western
> country in the last century. Such acceptance is really surprising
> in India, where the thriving indigenous theatre does not use

stage or auditorium. Or is that the reason – to keep theatre distinguished from Jatra, Tamasha, Bhawai and all the other 'native' entertainments? Is that the idea of sophistication on the part of city-theatre workers? Is it the city snobbery, born out of the dichotomy between the urban and rural areas of India due to the colonial character of the cities? . . . These questions and answers finally brought me to the task of exploring the possibilities of an alternative theatre – a Third Theatre. The thinking process has been substantiated by what I have seen of Jatra, Tamasha, Bhawai, Nautanki and Kathakali, of Chhou and Manipuri dances; and also by what I have seen in the theatre-in-the-round productions in London in 1957 and Paris in 1963, in the productions of Joan Littlewood in London, of Yuri Lyubimov in the Taganka Theatre in Moscow, in the Cinoherni Klub Theatre and the pantomime of Jari in Prague, in Grotowski's production of 'Apocalypsis cum Figuris' in his Theatre Laboratory in Wroclaw in Poland. It has been substantiated by discussions with various theatre personalities – Jerzy Grotowski, Julian Beck, Judith Malina, Richard Schechner and others.[4]

It will be clear, then, that influences on Sircar were not exclusively indigenous or exclusively Western, but that his choices were in-formed by experience of both.

Since the 1960s performance places for his plays have included the intimate setting of a room or small hall in buildings where audiences of only 100 or so have been able to watch, as well as outdoor venues such as Curzon Park, where Satabdi's productions in past years attracted a popular crowd of many thousands of spectators. In every case the direct communication between actors and specta-tors is established. If inside, then this means adapting the playing space of the auditorium to facilitate this.

One may interpret the rejection of the proscenium arch stage not only as a move towards a more flexible and intimate playing arena, but also as a refusal to be compromised by both the dramatic fare of bourgeois entertainment and the commercial ethos of the

---

4 Badal Sircar, *The Third Theatre*, Calcutta: Badal Sircar, 1978, p. 23.

inheritors of the colonial theatre in Calcutta. Nor is this anti-commercialism confined to a rejection of Western-style theatre. Sircar is equally scathing about the vast sums that the jatra performers make from their paying audiences. Sircar's move is unquestionably a move against the commercial values that may govern *any* performance.

The notion of the 'professional playwright' needs some careful scrutiny in an Indian context. If in the West the number of practising playwrights able to earn a living solely through their craft is small, in India it is minute, and now almost inevitably associated with the vast Indian film industry. Badal Sircar's training, and indeed his working life, was spent first as an engineer and then as a town planner, retiring as Director of Planning, Comprehensive Area Development Corporation, Calcutta in 1977. Similarly, the members of his theatre group Satabdi have continued to hold down jobs while pursuing rehearsals and giving performances in time after work and at weekends.

Grappling with the ideological aspects of the writer's function in a post-colonial society, several of Sircar's early plays feature an introspective central figure of poet-playwright, who is subjected, by various devices of self-examination, to an interrogation surrounding the writer's sense of personal worth, and his responsibility as initiator of change and development in the social organization of the community in which he lives. The enlarging radius of the sphere encompassing the notion of 'community' has been a part of Sircar's development as a writer and theatre practitioner.

The autobiographical aspects of these plays are difficult to ignore. One of the consistent features of Badal Sircar's writing is the tension that is created by the contradictions he experiences as an educated, professional, relatively affluent member of a middle-class community, detached and separated from the impoverished masses of India (and, by implication, the oppressed the world over). If the middle classes of India, and other former colonies for that matter, have not inherited the 'white man's burden', some may nevertheless have encountered at some time or another a fragmenting separation from the struggling lives of the vast majority of their compatriots, and shoulder a very real sense of responsibility for the continuance of this condition.

Sircar has confronted this sense of fragmentation frequently in his work, indeed it will be argued here that both the content and form of the plays reflect this dichotomy. An examination of several of his plays may be useful in locating and considering the theatrical means by which the central ideas of fragmentation and division find expression.

The early plays I deal with here lack solutions and refuse to do more than raise some of the contradictions by which Sircar is troubled. Both *Evam Indrajit* (1962) and *Shesh Nei* (1970) put the artist–writer on trial, in both literal and metaphorical senses, confronting some of the issues that have clearly been uppermost in Sircar's own consciousness.

In *Evam Indrajit*, Sircar draws several of the characters who people the imagination of the central figure of the Writer literally out from the audience. While the device is Pirandellian, Amal, Kamal, Vimal and Indrajit are more 'types' than characters, contemporaries caught up in the pursuit of middle-class ambitions of educational achievement, career moves, materialism and marriage prospects. As if to convey the arbitrariness of the routes through life that each takes, dialogue is used economically at key points to mark the stages of transition, with a flexible playing style that allows the actors to take on roles as required without regard for chronology, creating a fast-moving sequence of scenes. As an example of the style, here Indrajit struggles to keep pace with the college professor, variously played by Vimal and Kamal, who offers some defining terms:

The bell rings. AMAL *goes out.* INDRAJIT *stands up.* VIMAL *enters*
VIMAL: Roll Number Thirty-four!
INDRAJIT: Yes, Sir.
VIMAL: Poetry, in a general sense, may be defined to be 'the expression of imagination'.
The bell again. Exit VIMAL, KAMAL *enters*
KAMAL: Roll Number Thirty-four!
INDRAJIT: Yes, Sir.
KAMAL: The fundamental elements of the essay are logical development, expressive language, lucidity of thought and a balanced combination of theory and facts.

The bell. Exit KAMAL

INDRAJIT: A balanced combination of theory and facts. A balanced combination of theory and facts. Expression of the imagination. Expression of the imagination. (p. 7)

Knowledge and understanding are markedly different for Sircar, as Indrajit's parrot-fashion recitation of the principal points of the professor's definitions makes clear.

As young men, the quartet's discussions lean Westwards, to cricket, Hollywood filmstars Yul Brynner and Marlon Brando, and Einstein. Indrajit's encounter with the plays of George Bernard Shaw introduces a comparator against which the question of the place of politics in literature, in an Indian context, may be considered:

KAMAL: You know, our Pramatha Nath Bishi has also started writing plays like Shaw?
AMAL: Come on! Where's G.B.S. and where's P.N.B.?
VIMAL: Bishi loads his plays with politics.
KAMAL: And why not? There'll always be politics in literature. There should be!
AMAL: Come, come. Literature should embody all that's true, good and beautiful. It has nothing to do with politics. Politics is dirty.
VIMAL: Look, Brother, I object to 'dirty'. If Truth is dirty, ignoring it would be sheer escapism. Literature should be a reflection of life. Realistic. Don't you agree, Indrajit?
INDRAJIT: I'm not very clear actually. True, literature should be realistic. But to say it should be naked reflection of life ... (p. 9)

It is this lack of clarity, of singularity of definition of purpose to life, which is behind Indrajit's subsequent confession to the Writer that he wishes to 'go away', and the Writer's willingness to accompany him. The two are inextricably linked. The abandoning of responsibility towards a system that grinds on inexorably, dragging its willing victims between the twin stones of hope and ambition, as well as towards the bind of the writer struggling to come to terms with the function and meaning of art, are powerful if somewhat self-pitying impulses. The Writer feels misunderstood, not just by 'Auntie' whose periodic interruptions of his creative flow of scribbling with exhortations to eat properly, or get married, provide comic punctuation in the play, but by those who fail to share his vision of the endless 'Ferris wheel' of life, offering a simultaneity of promise and despair.

WRITER: I am divided. I am broken into pieces, into atoms. I'm a symphony composed of atoms.(p.29)

and again, here emphasizing both fragmentation and quest:

WRITER: I still think of Man, the whole Man, and the fragments of my consciousness are still searching – searching for something else. (p. 34)

For Indrajit, understanding of a kind is at least possible with his girlfriend and cousin Manasi, who correctly identifies his passion as anger, but finds her own temperament adjusted to acceptance and pity. Marriage between them seems impossible as long as Indrajit rejects her conventional 'rules' and she regards his extraordinariness as a bar. In any case, the Writer pessimistically refuses to write such a conjugation, preferring to emphasize the inevitability of the outcome whatever the choice: 'a circle – a zero'.

By the second act, Amal, Kamal, Vimal and Indrajit have assumed the bourgeois positions and junior managerial mantles they had been destined for, circulating files in endless, tedious repetition, broken only by the interruptions of the *chai wallah* for tea breaks. Their language is now unmistakably harking back to colonial banter:

AMAL: (*To* KAMAL) Hello Ghosh, old boy! Going to the club tonight?
VIMAL: I'm afraid not. My wife has invited a few old friends home.
KAMAL: Hello Ray, old boy! Have you got your car back from the garage yet?
INDRAJIT: No such luck. The clutch plate's burnt out, I'm told. Couldn't even get a taxi in time this morning. My servant took forty-five minutes to find one. (p. 32)

But Indrajit is still in touch with a consciousness of something beyond the humdrum of the routine he is now a part of, as the questioning of the Writer, together with his own doubts, makes plain. When, a notional seven years later, they meet up again it seems he has kept moving from job to job and still not yet married Manasi.

Typically, Sircar dissolves the exchange between Indrajit and the Writer to flash back to the parting of the ways with Manasi.

The device of the play being created by the Writer 'as it goes along' gives a 'present' quality to the action and allows opportunities for the characters to quiz their creator as to the progress of his play. The trio have also moved on, to educating their own children, arranging life insurance and taking out loans for business ventures. Indrajit, meanwhile, is bidding Manasi farewell, bound for London to pursue a course in engineering school (one of several autobiographical features in the play).

The third act – it will be noticed that *Evam Indrajit* was initially conceived for a conventional Western-style performance venue – begins with a card game in which Amal, Vimal and Kamal toss 'statements' out of a pack that is then reshuffled and dealt after each third turn. These statements reduce in scale from those of national significance ('On 15 August 1947 India became Independent', 'We escaped the clutches of the British Empire') to those of individual or personal anxiety ('Business is bad', 'My son failed again', 'My father has died'). This kind of structure is to become characteristic of Sircar's treatment of 'dialogue' in subsequent plays and, while it necessarily weakens an audience's engagement with character, such collaging may prove dramatically effective, either where tension is to be created through the presentation of contradictory views, or in the evocation of a particular locale, where shouts and cries emerge from a chorus to set a particular scene, be it on the street, in an office or on a crowded bus. Sometimes the disintegration of character is purposefully accomplished by this technique as when, during the Writer's final encounter with Indrajit, the trio mouth a miscellaneous selection of words, from 'isms' to ideologies, relations to occupations.

Indrajit has returned to the conventional life he had thought to evade and, now married, sees his life stretching ahead between the rails of a railway track which, no matter how far forward he moves, pushes the meeting point of the two lines on the horizon ever further into the distance. On the brink of finally accepting his 'ordinariness', of becoming Nirmal (normal?) the Writer once again intervenes to offer Indrajit 'the road':

WRITER: For us there is only the road. We shall walk. I know nothing to write about – still I shall have to write. You have nothing to say – still you will have to talk. Manasi has nothing to live for – she will have to live. For us there is only the road – so walk on. We are the cursed spirits of Sisyphus. We have to push the rock to the top – even if it just rolls down. (p. 59)

Such existential dilemmas, and the characters' self-conscious theatricality, are reminiscent of Beckett's 'we must go on, we can't go on', though here expressed in far less complex, more explicit terms.

Evam Indrajit already indicates Sircar's uninterest in the psychology of his dramatic characters. While the different kinds of responsibility facing the creative artist, and the frequent misunderstandings by others, provide one aspect of the play's theme, Sircar's construction of a special, symbiotic relationship between Indrajit and the Writer sets up a simple theatrical metaphor for the dialectic between the public and private selves of a single individual experiencing alienation from the expected norms of the society in which he finds himself. The play has been located in absurdist traditions, though the pessimism of the final note, as Indrajit's three contemporaries drift into the anonymity of conventional bourgeois existence, is muted by the redemptive power of a kind of conscientization the Writer manages to engender in his last remaining creation.

The central character of Sumanta in *Shesh Nei* (*There's No End*, 1970) is a young man whose fame has brought a multitude of fanatics to his house with garlands to fete his accomplishments and requests for autographs, pictures and interviews. Bewildered by the felicitations, he confides to his companion Sumati his feelings of unease, of anticipation of some flaw in his character that must surely signal impending doom. When finally alone, Sumanta is confronted by an unnamed diabolic figure, called simply 'The Man', who commands him to attend his own trial, Kafkaesquely refusing to explain precisely what charges are to be brought. It is eventually through hypnosis that Sumanta is brought to the dock.

The stage is then converted to present a trial setting. The Man assumes the role of chief prosecutor and presents his case against Sumanta in front of an imagined judge and jury, symbolized by chairs set down by other actors, with wigs, gavel and law books positioned on a central table. What follows is a procession of witnesses, beginning with his mother, to give evidence to 'the court' in his trial.

Where in *Evam Indrajit* the Writer/Indrajit fracture the self in two, finally to be drawn together in conclusion, *Shesh Nei* theatricalizes the ontological insecurities of Sumanta to present archetypal figures of mother, boss, fiancée, teacher, and revolutionary engaged in confrontation with, and accusation against, the young writer. It may be somewhat paradoxical that, as has already been mentioned, though Sircar's interest in the psychological roundedness of his dramatic creations is minimal, both plays may be seen to serve as critical self-examinations of his personal psychology. It is particularly interesting in this play that hypnosis – a traditional gateway to the unconscious – is used to bring about the trial, inevitably reminiscent of the famous final act of Leopold Lewis's melodrama *The Bells*, where a dream mesmerist elicits a confession from the conscience-racked murderer Mathias, to prompt a self-administered sentence.

Each of the figures drawn to give evidence in Sumanta's trial brings a different accusation. His mother believes her son wilfully fell into the clutches of the wrong kind of girl; Manika (the girl in question), accuses him of cheating on her, though she loved him in spite of their lack of a common education, culture or class; his college professor claims he gave up the opportunity of a useful research career and that science had expected much more of him; his erstwhile boss accuses him of having to be sacked because of his drunken behaviour. Prasanta Das, sometime friend, ally, political activist and revolutionary, presents perhaps the most interesting accusation:

THE MAN: How has he harmed you?
PRASANTA: That's my personal affair.
THE MAN: There's no such thing as a personal affair in court. Remember – the whole truth.
PRASANTA: (*after a pause*) He murdered my only friend.
THE MAN: (*jumps at it*) Got you! Murder! Milord! Gentlemen of the jury! Please take note! Murder! Who did he kill? What is the name of the person he murdered?
PRASANTA: Sumanta Sanyal. (p. 7)

Here, the 'crime' carries a double meaning of murder and suicide, both signifying the sense of betrayal with which Prasanta wishes to confront Sumanta. The revolutionary is an absurd, posturing figure, but the centrality of the 'failed commitment' in political aspects of life is matched by the rehearsal of failed personal relationships with Mrinalini (Sumanta's mother), Manika and, to a lesser extent, Sumati. Sumati is close to *Evam Indrajit*'s Manasi in being an articulate woman friend who at least makes some attempt to understand Sumanta's impulse to write, and rejects the demands of allegiance and accusations of betrayal voiced by the others. She refuses to co-operate with the prosecutor, explaining: 'Sumanta is trying to find himself – searching, probing. He has at last found himself – has finally realised himself in his poetry, in his writings' (p. 15). She recognizes, however, that his love for her and his poetry fail to address the 'gap' she sees within his romanticized vision, and it is at this point that the ghosts of his conscience emerge in the shape of five witnesses, universal victims: the bastee-dweller, the victim of communal riots, the nuclear dead, the dying muse of poetry, and the blind.

Ultimately Sumanta acknowledges his responsibilities as a writer, rejecting the codes that have framed his relationships of the past. He assumes the part of the judge in the final moments of the play, reversing the accusation to implicate the prosecutor, and indeed all of the characters, who now assume the role of the jury. Admitting that they are all 'the accused', Sumanta explains that the verdict is open, but the trial is not over, there is no end to the trial.

The theatrical form Sircar adopts in *Shesh Nei* allows a central figure to dialogue with parts of a fractured self, responding to allegations presented by 'witnesses' in a trial structure. This giving of evidence also permits the now familiar flashback or re-presentation of past events that throw light on Sumanta's present crisis, such as the day of the riot all those years ago when the political ambitions of middle-class youth proved insufficient to mobilize a more sceptical proletariat. However, perhaps this device is underused here, since the trial runs out of dramatic steam as the procession of witnesses proves repetitive, the significance of the testimonies loses impact, and a sense of engagement with the confrontation diminishes.

In many ways Sircar's theatre form since these early plays has become inextricably linked to the notion that the message is more important than the aesthetic means by which it is conveyed. In this sense his theatre is 'poor', stripped of any excesses of decorative embellishment, elaborate costumes, scenery, lights and so on. *Sagino Mahato* (1971) represented a departure from his previous work and was the first of many plays to be produced in this 'poor' style by Sircar's theatre group Satabdi. It charts the rise and fall of a committed worker attempting to achieve improvements in the working conditions of his colleagues.

Sircar discusses the important transition *Sagino Mahato* made from proscenium arch to arena staging in *The Third Theatre*:

> The first experimental production of the play outside the proscenium theatre took place on 24th October 1971 at the All Bengal Teachers' Association hall in Calcutta. It is a small hall with a tiny stage on one side, seating about 200 poeple when used as a conventional auditorium. We arranged the chairs in the hall and also on the stage in such a manner that a central arena is obtained for acting. But we did not restrict the production to arena-acting or 'theatre-in-the-round'. There were passages behind the spectators used for movements and acting. Thus the separation of the spectators from the performers was further broken, and a sense of being within the performance was imparted which could induce a considerable degree of involvement. (p. 27)

During the aforementioned performance an electric fuse blew the lighting circuit and plunged the stage into darkness at a critical moment. The actors kept going, but when the house lights went on again and the audience kept its attention, Sircar came to the realization that elaborate lighting effects were by no means essential to the kind of production he was evolving.

Subsequently, Sircar's adaptation of Howard Fast's novel *Spartacus* (1973) proved to be greatly enhanced by the powerful theatrical simplicity of its staging, whether performed inside or outside, with the Satabdi actors choreographed into a striking physicality to convey the toil of the Romans' slaves, rhythmically accompanied by *dhol* (drum) percussion and song, by now ubiquitous features of Sircar's plays. Confrontation with authoritarian systems of oppression are of primary thematic concern in these plays.

Sircar's use of chorus is vital, stressing not only the universal nature of the 'characters' he creates in his plays, as the actors fluidly take on roles and then merge back into the group, but exemplifying yet again the fragmented collage of perspectives and identities, now beginning to find some kind of focus, at least in conclusion.

Michhil (Procession, 1974) has been an immensely successful play, using the noisy, chaotic evocation of Calcutta's crowded streets in a theatrical setting that incorporates an audience arranged informally around the acting arena, in a fast-moving, satirical tragi-comedy of police repression, establishment hypocrisy, race riot and personal loss of direction. Here the audience is continually engaged by a bombardment of sound and action from the chorus (now simply numbered One, Two, Three, etc.) from the very outset of the play, when the lights go out and amid the confusion of the blackout (Satabdi have often performed out of doors where it is still possible to convey this by the actors 'playing blind') a piercing death scream rises up.

Khoka, the murdered young man, reappears many times as the play proceeds, the everyman victim, unseen by the forces of authority, initially represented in the figure of the Officer who bawls the chattering chorus to silence each time they question among themselves the circumstances of Khoka's disappearance. Sircar imaginatively exploits the comic potential of Khoka's continual death and resurrection, setting this against the mundane urban routines of daily life where snatches of colloquial conversation evoke a crowded bus, the dryness of newspaper and media bulletins, persuasive hawkers selling their wares on the street corner or in the marketplace, a factory siren's call to work, or the frenzied financial exchange of the dealing room.

As the search for Khoka is about to commence, an old man (invariably played by Badal Sircar himself), who has entered the acting arena describes the beginnings of his own 'search':

OLD MAN: When I was small, very small, one day, one morning, half-way between fall and winter, a sweet morning made of a chill in the air and sunshine dripping with sweetness, I walked along the road, holding on to my father. I trampled dry leaves crunching under my feet, as I was filled with the smell of rotting leaves, wild flowers and the slushy earth. I held on to my father's hands, as the road wound and meandered along and receded under my feet giving place to yet new roads. (*He begins to walk.*) All the roads vanished beyond the bend till a new road flashed at the bend till it vanished again at the next bend and a new one again and a bend and the vanishing road the new road the ro-o-o-ad. (*He stops.*) Then father said, Khoka, let's go back. I said, Just a little more till the next bend and I have a look beyond the bend . . . (p. 8)

This is a fine piece of storytelling, as the images conjured are reinforced by points at which the Old Man begins to walk or stops, as well as establishing a kind of temporal elasticity, a connectedness between generations and the earth. In the Old Man's revelation that his name is also Khoka, we are presented with another of Sircar's fragmentations of his plays' central figure. The 'road' the Old Man is following is surely one and the same as that upon which Indrajit and the Writer are about to set out at the end of *Evam Indrajit*. But the significant difference between the Writer/Indrajit and the Old Man/ Khoka is that a duality has now been established with the *victim*. This is more complex than Sumanta's encounter with the ghosts of his conscience, and certainly far more theatrically interesting in the way that it is handled.

The image of the procession in *Michhil* is employed to present both negative and positive aspects of the joining together of individuals and communities under a common banner. What is at issue is not the desirability of such an endeavour, but the nature of the banner under which the processing throng sets off. Sircar parodies blind faith in religion, sloganeering for its own sake, communalism and markets of whatever hue:

CHORUS: Glory be to the Lord Krishna, incarnation of the markets. We bow at the feet of the Lord Blackmarket. Hail to the Black god. The Black god will save us all. Vote for Mr Blackie Marketwala. Vote for Mr Blackie Marketwala. (p. 21)

The rhetoric of power from the mouths of religious leaders, politicians or from along the corridors of bureaucratic offices is placed in disturbing and ironic juxtaposition with the awful whine of the (ignored) beggar woman appealing for bread. Such sound collages have a poetic intensity about them, yet Sircar's intention is never a purely aesthetic one.

The conclusion of *Michhil* unites the two Khokas, dead and alive, past and present, young and old, lost and found, victim and conscientized. In an enormously optimistic and rousing conclusion, the chorus link hands to form a 'procession of dreams' around the acting arena, joined by the Khokas who invite those members of the audience who would like to do so to follow on in a singing procession. The proximity of the audience, though akin to jatra, now facilitates a direct contact and engagement between actors and spectators, who are not passive recipients of thrilling entertainment but active participants in a living drama.

So much of Badal Sircar's development as a writer and theatre practitioner has evolved as a result of his passionate belief in the medium of a 'free' theatre, as being the most direct means of conveying Satabdi's work to the widest possible audience. Sircar's theatre is 'free' in two senses: it is liberated from the constraints of Western theatre's naturalistic expectation, and literally free for its audiences, who are expected to pay only what they can afford. His mistrust of any notion of commercialism within his theatre means that Satabdi has always been known as 'the group' and never his 'company'.

One of the aspects of the group's work has been in discovering and performing for non-urban audiences, and over the years Sircar has helped organize *parikrama*, or shows taken to the rural areas, in the Sundarbans and other Bengali districts. Plays such as *Bhoma* (1976) have been created, which confront rural and urban audiences alike with the vast difference between the lives of impoverished villagers and the well-heeled city dwellers.

Sircar points out in his preface to the play, 'there is no character, no story, no continuity'. What we have in place of these is a series of chorus-created scenes that alternate between city preoccupations and the concerns of the forest villagers. Interweaving themes bind these worlds together: the place of love, humankind's in-humanity ('Is human blood warm or cold?' ask the chorus repeatedly), usury and its impact on agricultural development, Third World debt, the atomic sword of Damocles, and the calamities of flood and famine. Indeed, it might be argued that there are far too many issues raised for the strength of the play to bear. One worthy of mention in a post-colonial context is the following jaundiced view of the conse-quences of a good middle-class Indian education:

FOUR: Your country will also sell its pots and pans to educate him.
FIVE: Thousands of pots and pans will be spent to educate him.
SIX: Educated, he will depart in glory for America.
TWO: I'll get his picture printed in the newspapers.
THREE: Your son will earn thousands of dollars in America.
FOUR: You'll advertise in the papers for a bride for your son in America.
FIVE: Meanwhile your son will have married a blue-eyed American blonde. (p. 68)

However, at the play's core is Bhoma, variously defined by the chorus at different points as individual ('When Bhoma was sixteen he came to clear the forest'), collective ('Bhoma is the village'), and cultural ('Bhoma is the jungle, Bhoma is the cornfield') icon. While undoubtedly still conveying a sense of personal victim, in *Bhoma* Khoka's oppression is abstracted a stage further to encompass the forces of disintegration acting on both individual and cultural identity. At the play's end Bhoma, hungry and exploited, rises up and strikes out with sharpened axe against the 'poisonous forests', as the chorus mime together their energetic continuation of struggle.

The harnessing of a people's collective will in opposition to forces of oppression (however hopeless the task may seem), and their focus into acts of resistance along an historical continuum, become key components of *Basi Khabar* (*Stale News*), devised by Satabdi in 1979. This agitprop, pseudo-documentary drama takes the revolt of the Santhali tribal people against British colonial rule in 1855 as its starting point. The background to the uprising, the revolt and its aftermath of repressive retribution are presented in epic style by a chorus of eight actors, driven in narrative explication by the conscientizing encounter of one of their number with a symbolic, unvanquished Santhali, swathed from head to foot in bandages and moving silently between their ranks: the Dead Man. The victim figure here is powerful dramatically, not simply because of his costuming but principally because, though he is mute, it is through his intervention that the story of his people is told by the chorus.

Characteristically, the target in all this is not, fundamentally, colonialism's evils: *dikus* (money lenders), *naib-suzawals* (rent collectors), landholders and corrupt police officers, among others, must also take their share of responsibility. The Dead Man 'speaks' (in silence) to a future generation, a post-colonial, urban generation, bearing witness to the sufferings of the past, but in so doing demonstrating the injustices of the present. While *Basi Khabar* is far too overloaded with indigestible factual material (betraying its group devised origins), which impedes the dramatic impetus of the Santhals' story, it may be seen as a logical development from *Bhoma*, with a contemporary, urban Indian society's interest in re-evaluating the nature of its relationship with an exploited tribal one culminating in its final rallying call to 'scream'.

Badal Sircar resolutely refuses to offer practical solutions, spell out an agenda for political reform, or define precisely what is entailed by the scream. What does he expect of his audiences? How should they react to this unstoppable porcupine of conscience pricking? It almost feels at times as though in his writing Sircar has absorbed the jatra character of the Vivek. Indeed, his plays are littered with characters and choruses who confront and question human action: the Writer, Sumanta's ghosts, Khoka in all his guises, the Dead Man.

Unsurprisingly, Sircar has drawn fire from those who feel that the continual banging of the drum and piping of the same tune leads down an ideological, not to mention theatrical, cul-de-sac. Is Badal Sircar simply a well-intentioned but naive idealist who as protesting playwright speaks more of his own middle-class guilt than about positioning attainable marker posts on the path towards a distant Marxist paradise? A paradise where there is sharing not share holding, righteousness but not religion, co-operation replacing conflict, peace not private property, and where ethical cleansing triumphs over its ethnic equivalent?

It is just such a utopia that Sircar's two thieves, Kena and Becha, find themselves in, having been submerged in a river during their flight from irate pursuers in *Hattamalar Oparey* (*Beyond the Land of Hattamala*, 1977). The land that they arrive in has abolished not only money but private property, crime, the police, hunger, abuse and aggression of all kinds. This provides some wonderful comic moments as the thieves encounter a topsy-turvy society, an inverse image of their own, and struggle to comprehend the fact that the absence of the market makes their profession quite redundant and provides them with plenty: who needs to steal gold when it can be borrowed from the library? As the thieves decide to make the place their home, the fantasy is complete.

Sircar is familiar with all the criticisms, but sees no reason why he should have to defend himself against those who suggest that he should pursue any other course than that to which his life has been committed. He is one of a generation (now being lost), which came of age with India's unshackling from its colonial yoke, engraved with the contradictions of his parents' education, language and religion, yet better placed that any generation of Indians to redeem the pledge on the stroke of the midnight hour, as Jawaharlal Pandit Nehru's promised tryst with destiny arrived. It is hardly surprising that idealism is a driving force behind such a collage of contradictory images finding expression in the fragmenting forms of his work, either at the outset of the journey in the self-interrogation of the purpose of the writer's craft, halfway along the road in the overlaying of themes exploring notions of victim and oppressor, or still further on with a utopian vision of change. Throughout, the constants have been the physically expressive, chorus-based theatre practice, the honesty of communication with the audience, the sincerity of the performers (who have consistently eschewed any financial or personal gain from the work), and the immediacy and directness of the performance.

Fundamentally, Sircar continues to regard himself not as a playwright, fashioning his work to suit the critical tastes of a sophisticated urban audience, and certainly not as a politician, but as a 'theatre man', very much part of a movement that has gathered momentum over time. In this respect his ambition has long been to reach the 'real' audience of India: the villagers. Increasingly this is happening not through the performance of his plays – Sircar would now acknowledge that Satabdi has passed its zenith – but through his leading of workshops that have sought to liberate the emotions and creativity of the participants, however unfamiliar they may be with 'theatre' or his working process. The trust and enthusiasm that Badal Sircar is able to engender within the workshop situation and the obstacles to expression he dismantles, are functions of an unswerving honesty and integrity, qualities that others have envied, and few in an Indian, or for that matter any other, context have matched.

Girish Karnad and an Indian theatre of roots

It is most significant that Suresh Awasthi, former chair of the National School of Drama, former general secretary of Sangeet Natak Akademi, locates the crucial starting point of the development of an Indian 'theatre of roots' in B. V. Karanth's direction of a new play by Girish Karnad in 1972:

> Girish Karnad's famous *Hayavadana*, inspired by the yakshagana of Karnataka, begins with the prayer 'Jai Gajavadane' – 'Victory to Ganesha', the elephant-headed god – and its innovative and improvisatory production ... with music, mime, and movements heralded the return of Lord Ganesha, the presiding deity of traditional theatre. With this event, we might say, contemporary theatre began its encounter with tradition.[1]

Born in 1938 in Matheran near Bombay, Karnad has described himself as belonging to the first generation of playwrights to come of age after India became independent. Although he was to move to Bombay for his postgraduate studies, his childhood was spent growing up in a small village in Karnataka. At this time he remembers watching two kinds of theatre: touring productions put on by troupes

---

* Plays in English translation referred to in this chapter are as follows: *Tughlaq*, Madras: Oxford University Press, 1972; *Hayavadana*, Calcutta: Oxford University Press, 1975; *Nāga-Mandala*, New Delhi: Oxford University Press, 1990; *Talé-daṇḍa*, New Delhi: Ravi Dayal Publisher, 1993.

[1] Suresh Awasthi, '"Theatre of Roots", Encounter with Tradition', *TDR*, 33:4 (T124), p. 49.

of professional actors in *natak* companies, and folk theatre performances of *yakshagana*. These will be outlined in due course, since
an understanding of their characteristic features will usefully inform
an examination of how indigenous traditions of performance have
been incorporated into contemporary post-colonial playwriting in
India. Girish Karnad was later to turn to both forms in his playwriting, though, like several of the writers included in this volume,
his early influences and experimentation were based on an exposure
to Western plays and modes of theatre practice.

In Bombay, for example, Karnad recalls watching Ebrahim
Alkazi's production of Strindberg's *Miss Julie* and describes the
impact of the control of stage lighting. In contrast to the open air
experience of Karnataka's rural theatre, the manipulation of the
scenic space with light illustrated not only the possibility of the
creation of interior and exterior space along naturalistic lines, but the
exploration of character psyche, the revelation of emotional states
and the inner workings of the mind.

Like Sircar and Soyinka, Karnad was to come to England to
continue his education after schooling, and at more or less the same
time. As for the other writers, this period abroad was to prove
formative in Karnad's re-examination of his cultural background and
its relationship with his creative writing. In fact it was in 1960, while
still in India and in anticipation of taking up a three-year scholarship
in England (he was Rhodes Scholar at Magdalen College, Oxford), that
Karnad began writing a play that was written not in English, the
language of his education, but in Kannada, the regional language of
Karnataka. The theme of the play was a story taken from the Hindu
epic *Mahabharata*, from which he then considered himself alienated.

The play, called *Yayati*, has not been published in English, but
is a reinterpretation of the myth of King Yayati, an early ancestor of
the Kuru dynasty. The king is cursed to old age as a consequence of
an adulterous affair with his queen Devayani's maid, Sharmishtha.
Yayati's pleas for mitigation to the gods result in the commutation of
the curse, enabling him (not unlike Admetus in the Greek myth of a
similar nature that Euripides used in writing *Alcestis*), to seek
another person with whom to exchange his old age. This proves to be
his own son, Puru.

Karnad departs from the myth in respect of the fact that he chooses not to make Puru the product of Yayati's union with Sharmishtha, but his son by an earlier marriage to an Asura princess. This is in order to emphasize Puru's personal choice of self-sacrifice, rather than as atonement for his father's sin. Yet unlike the tranquil end of the myth, where Yayati finally comes to the realization that enjoying physical happiness does not result in ultimate satisfaction and returns his youth to Puru, Karnad's play ends tragically in death and sacrifice.

In retrospect, on the verge of a departure for England and the excitement of beginning a new and independent life, Girish Karnad has articulated the particular relevance of the myth to his own situation, when anxieties within his family were being expressed about his failure to follow expected routes towards career and marriage.

Yet the central difficulty was in finding an appropriate theatrical form in which to express his interest in the mythology. Although inspired by Ebrahim Alkazi's productions of Strindberg and Anouilh, the question became one of how he might use the dramatic medium in his own way, not merely in imitation of Western dramatists:

> A playwright needs a tradition he can call his own, even if it is only to reject it. Anouilh could refer to Greek tragedy and its neo-classical reincarnation as well as the theatre of occupied France. I could only imitate Anouilh, for there was nothing to refer to: the *natak* companies and *yakshagana* seemed to belong to another world altogether. Nothing filled the void they had left.[2]

It is interesting here that in spite of his firsthand childhood experience of the indigenous regional folk theatre of Karnataka, it did not occur to Karnad then to regard this as a tradition of which he might prove inheritor. There are, perhaps, several reasons why this may have been the case. Class difference may have played a part: what connection might a young, English, medium-educated, middle-class

---

[2] Girish Karnad, 'Theatre in India', *Daedalus*, 118:4 (Fall 1989), p. 334.

academic have with an itinerant troupe of performers travelling from village to village in rural Karnataka by bullock cart? Yakshagana, like so many folk forms, depends on the improvisational skills of its performers, not the performance of scripted roles. These performers often pass their skills from one generation to another and are not dependent on an external, organizing agent. Similarly, the inclusion of music, song and dance must have seemed beyond the province of a playwright imbued with the preoccupations of psychological realism and characters engaged in existential dilemmas, along the lines of the Western theatrical models of the time provided by Beckett, Anouilh or Sartre. Perhaps, fundamentally, it was felt that the theatrical forms of indigenous models were insufficiently 'worthy' to bear the weight of the serious issues that Karnad wished to address. In any event the experience of a cultural dislocation is evident, as the primary currency of theatre practice seemed valued in Western terms while the themes and ideas for dramatic treatment sprang from India's historical and mythological past.

Karnad's time abroad engendered quite different views from those he left India with, and, though he was unable to devote himself fully to playwriting during his studies, he was becoming convinced that Western theatre forms had little to offer him personally in his theatre writing. It was to the natak companies of his childhood that he turned.

The natak companies' plays followed the structure of the original Parsi theatre productions. The Parsis, followers of the Zoroastrian religion and ethnically quite distinct, first settled on the west coast of India more than a millennium ago, after migration from present-day Iran. Now concentrated primarily in Bombay and Gujerat, they were to become the most highly Western-educated section of nineteenth-century Indian society, taking key roles in British colonial administration of the country.

In Bombay the Parsi community had, since the mid-nineteenth century, established a supremacy in the presentation of secular musical dramas that drew on Hindu myths, as well as adaptations of foreign romances. Adapting to the changing prevalence of the cultural milieu over time, they were presented in a number of languages during their years of popularity, beginning with English, followed by

Gujerati and finally Hindi. As with the music hall in Britain in the 1930s, and at about the same time, the Parsi theatre was irrevocably depleted as a consequence of the mass audiences drawn by the burgeoning film industry. India's film industry, of course, continues to this day to be one of the world's most powerful and commercially successful, and has a profound impact on traditional theatre forms, whether folk or classical.

Tughlaq was written in Kannada and completed in 1964 after Girish Karnad's return to India from England. Where *Yayati* had been constructed around the reworking of a myth, in this play Karnad's attention turned again to 'roots', but this time of a primarily historical rather than mythological kind, in the form of the most controversial figure in the turbulent history of the Delhi sultanate, the fourteenth-century ruler Muhammad ud Din Tughlaq.

Tughlaq is remembered for his brutality, his expansionist policy, particularly in ill-fated expeditions against the Mongols and into Afghanistan, his introduction of a token currency in brass and copper, which was rejected by the troops he sought to pay with it, and, chiefly, his catastrophic decision in 1327 to shift his expanding empire's capital from Delhi to Daulatabad in the Deccan, a decision subsequently reversed only a few years later. Historians have held conflicting views over whether it was a case of Tughlaq's considered political ambitions simply proving beyond him, or whether, Nero-like, his own whimsicality and madness were responsible for the disasters that befell his reign.

This ambiguity of historical interpretation is something of which Karnad is acutely conscious, and exploits, in his characterization of the king. On one level Tughlaq is a scheming despot who despatches his enemies, including his own kith and kin (we understand from action that has taken place prior to the start of the play), with terrifying calculation. His distracted air as he ponders a chess problem while his childhood friend Ain-ul-Mulk and his army of thirty thousand approach Delhi, conceals a sabre-sharp intellect capable of finding solutions to many problems simultaneously. Tughlaq is unpredictable and dangerous because of his capacity to remain one step ahead of the opposition at all times. His character, as with so many similar dramatic creations from Richard III to the villains of the melodramatic stage, is indisputably magnetic and alluring.

Structurally, Karnad has explained that he incorporated in *Tughlaq* aspects of natak productions he had seen as a boy. The natak companies, which largely declined after the movies arrived, were simply touring troupes of professional actors who performed on semi-permanent 'end-on' proscenium stages, with simple wings and back-drops. For evening shows the stage would be lit in a rudimentary way by paraffin lamps, which allowed little in the way of lighting control. In these natak plays the presentation of scenes downstage in front of a curtain ('shallow scenes') would be alternated with those that used the full stage ('deep scenes'). Traditionally, the 'shallow scenes' featured comic interludes, perhaps in front of a street scene, having a functional purpose in allowing time to prepare the set behind the curtain for the more elaborate 'serious' settings that followed. In *Tughlaq* just such a pattern of scene alternation is established. However, rather than remaining separate, the 'low-life' characters of the fore-stage, specifically the comic double-act pairing of Aazam and Aziz, become intrinsically involved with the 'main-stage' action of the sultan's court.

While there are many comic exchanges between the pair, particularly early on as a consequence of the Muslim *dhobi* (laundry-man) Azim's irreverent disguise as a Brahmin to further his fraudulent claim against dispossession of his land, as the play proceeds the comedy turns a darker shade. Aziz adopts the worst excesses of exploitation in the treatment meted out to the stragglers on the road to Daulatabad, in lethal combination with a political – and religious – cynicism that leads to the kidnapping, killing and impersonation of a holy man destined for Tughlaq's court. Aziz's skills at role-playing are matched only by the sultan himself.

Like many dramatists who choose to locate contemporary concerns in an historical setting, Girish Karnad has been unwilling to make overt reference to contemporary political figures and incidents that may have been in his mind in writing the play, and this is certainly not necessary for an appreciation of *Tughlaq*. Though he has indicated, and any experience of the play will make it clear, that it is far more than a costume drama:

What struck me absolutely about Tughlaq's history was that it was contemporary ... within a span of twenty one years this tremendously capable man had gone to pieces. This seemed to be both due to his idealism as well as the shortcomings within him, such as his impatience, his cruelty, his feeling that he had the only correct answer. And I felt in the early sixties India had also come very far in the same direction – the twenty-year period seemed to me very much a striking parallel. [3]

The fact that Jawaharlal Nehru's long period of prime ministerial office (1947–64) coincides with that twenty-year span invites us to make a connection, though it would be too easy to over-simplify Karnad's interest, which isn't, after all, in examining the psychology of a dominant political figure, but in considering the way in which *history is made*, not only through the influence of a central power, but through the participation in its perpetuation of those on the margins of such power.

History-making shares much in common with myth-making, and Tughlaq is always conscious of posterity's view of his actions. It is interesting that the sultan's two chief counsellors are given the professions they have. Najib is a politician: constantly attuned to the art of the possible in the here and now, and ultimately murdered by Tughlaq's stepmother in the kind of political manoeuvring of which he himself has been prime exponent. Barani, the historian, seems to possess sole licence to criticize the sultan by virtue not only of the wisdom and authority his study of the past has granted him, but in the symbolic position he occupies as bearer of the record of the sultan's deeds to future generations. Here is a case in point where, on the ramparts of the fort in Daulatabad some five years after the action of the first half of the play, Muhammad, besieged on all sides by drought, uprisings and the currency crisis, seeks advice:

MUHAMMAD: What should I do, Barani? What would you prescribe for this honeycomb of diseases? I have tried everything. But what cures one disease just worsens another.

---

[3] Interview in *Enact*, June 1971, cited in U. R. Anantha Murthy, 'Introduction', *Tughlaq*, Madras: Oxford University Press, 1972, p. viii.

BARANI: I am a humble historian, Your Majesty: it's not for me to prescribe. But since Your Majesty has done me the honour of confiding in me, may I make a suggestion? It is a difficult thing to suggest to a king and I beg you to forgive me if it hurts. But you are a learned man, Your Majesty, you are known the world over for your knowledge of philosophy and poetry. History is not only made in statecraft; its lasting results are produced in the ranks of learned men. That's where you belong, Your Majesty, in the company of learned men. Not in the market of corpses. (*Tughlaq*, p. 55)

But this invitation to retire from the throne, to abandon the savagery and torture that have come to characterize his rule, is dependent on a volte-face which Tughlaq is not prepared to countenance:

MUHAMMAD: But for all that I'll have to admit I've been wrong all these years. And I know I haven't. I have something to give, something to teach, which may open the eyes of history. (*Tughlaq*, p.56)

The relationship between Tughlaq and Barani, ruler and historian, is a central one in the play. Yet Karnad is at pains to make it clear that Barani is more than a merely allegorical figure, and that he has some connection to the life beyond the walls of the fort where he has become increasingly embroiled and complicit in the violence and repression of the sultan's rule. His decision to leave, to return to the scene of his own mother's butchering by Tughlaq's soldiers in yet another quashing of popular insurrection, might suggest a measure of understanding of the brutal cost of Tughlaq's power. Yet in leaving, Barani fails to see that Tughlaq's final confrontation with Aziz, who has so skilfully and cynically manipulated all in his path to now dizzying heights of power, is a meeting of a man with his own reflection. Aziz is awarded a state office by Tughlaq with inescapable logic, but ultimately it is the sultan who 'loses himself' as he determines to take his court back to Delhi and the realization dawns that the 'history' he had sought to extend his control over will chart its own course.

In a letter to Pratibha Agrawal of 25 October 1970, Girish Karnad announced the completion of a new play called *Hayavadana*. Where *Yayati* had used *Mahabharata* mythology and Western dramatic form, *Tughlaq* medieval Indian history and scenic conventions of natak companies (though without the ubiquitous dance and song of their productions), *Hayavadana* demonstrated yet another approach:

> Technically it's a departure for me, since I have used many of the techniques of local folk theatre – ... entry curtains, songs etc. But I doubt if I could have even thought of this play if I hadn't been involved with *Evam Indrajit*. The open, fluid form of Sircar's play changed, or rather expanded, my feeling for the stage enormously.[4]

A discussion of *Evam Indrajit* is made elsewhere (in the chapter on Badal Sircar), and although the two dramatists have followed very different paths in their playwriting it is evident that the process of getting to know the play through its translation for production by the Madras Players in 1970, which he also directed, proved inspirational for Girish Karnad.

In many ways *Hayavadana* represents a perfect synthesis of folk theatre performance traditions, Indian mythology and thematic contemporaneity, though, paradoxically, Karnad's point of departure was a short story by the Nobel prize-winning German author Thomas Mann entitled *The Transposed Heads*, which was itself taken from a traditional Indian riddle in the anthology *Vetalapanchavimshati-katha*.

The central story's adaptation follows the plotting of *The Transposed Heads* quite closely, and may be described briefly. A young Brahmin falls in love with a beautiful girl and his blacksmith friend agrees to act as go-between for the couple. They subsequently marry. But later, during a stopover on a cart journey, the Brahmin youth visits a Kali temple where he offers himself to the goddess as a sacrifice, cutting off his own head. The blacksmith, going in search of his friend, discovers his body at the temple and, out of loyalty (as well as fearing accusations of impropriety in his intentions towards his friend's wife), follows sacrificial suit. On finding the two dead, the girl is prevented from her own suicide by the intervention of the goddess,

---

[4] Interview with Pratibha Agrawal, 17 February 1982 in *Rangvarta*, 51, February 1991, p. 12.

who grants the boon of resurrection, only for the girl to reattach the heads to the wrong bodies. The question as to which is now her husband is resolved by a hermit, who declares that the head rules the body, therefore the husband must be the body with the Brahmin's head. It now seems the girl has the best of both worlds, since the Brahmin's mind is complemented by the blacksmith's physical prowess, which she had long admired. Yet what follows is a gradual reversion of the bodies to their original forms. Dreaming once again of the blacksmith, the girl, together with her child, sets off for the forest where he has taken refuge, pursued by her husband. The story ends in bloodshed as the two friends agree to fight to the death, and the girl, believing her son's social position will suffer if she fails in her duty, commits *sati*.

seemingly perfect combination of 2 bodies

The centrality of the philosophical problem posed by the search for completeness is reinforced in Karnad's *Hayavadana* through his framing of the main action of the play, which follows the outline above, by a secondary story that features the eponymous horse-man hero, Hayavadana. The product of a union between the Princess of Karnataka and a *ghandarva* (celestial being) cursed to a horse's form, Hayavadana has a human body and a horse's head. His quest for (human) completeness is ultimately resolved at the play's conclusion when he returns, again through divine intervention, now complete: a complete horse. This cleverly mirrors, and parodies, the exchanged heads of the main story, which subsequently exert their influence over the human bodies that each finds itself atop.

Karnad's use of particular conventions drawn from the yaksha-gana folk theatre contribute in many ways to the overall style of the play. It would be appropriate here to examine in more detail some of the characteristics of the performance tradition in order to see how this has been achieved.

The word yakshagana derives from *yaksha*, which means 'demi-gods', and *gana*, which means 'song'. A play text survives from the mid-sixteenth century, though the origins of yakshagana must predate this. The most performed extant plays, or *prasangas*, number more than 100, and are mostly adapted from episodes taken from the Hindu epics *Ramayana* and *Mahabharata*. The tales enacted feature demons, heroes and gods, often making devotional journeys, engaged

song to coverup a short story

in securing marriage partnerships, avenging conflict, giving battle, vanquishing evil, or ultimately reconciling differences. Texts are written in Kannada, the language of Karnataka, prefaced by a sung prologue, often in Sanskrit, the high caste language of classical Indian theatre. Throughout, the evocation of *rasa*, the aesthetic 'flavour' or emotional quality derived from the performance by the audience as specific to the episode being performed, is aimed at by the performers. The rasa or moods of yakshagana are often of a passionate or violent kind.

Given the long history of the tradition it will be evident that innumerable changes and influences have occurred over the time that yakshagana has been practised. Yet there are common elements that have endured. Each troupe, with a repertoire of a score or more of plays, travels from village to village in a season that begins in November and ends in May. Plays are now frequently performed at the behest of private patronage rather than in the temple settings where they had their traditional setting. The outdoor physical space in which the play is to be performed is marked out as a sixteen-feet square, with a pole fixed at each of the four corners. On top of the poles is tied a colourful canopy decorated with a kind of bunting of feathers, leaves and coloured paper. The audience sits on three sides of the performance space. The play begins after nine in the evening and continues all night until dawn.

Yakshagana begins with invocatory rituals to Ganesha, a garlanded statue of whom is kept in the 'green room' by the actors throughout the performance, followed by a sung prologue. A musical director, called the *bhagavata*, not only beats time with his cymbals as he begins to sing of the first episode from the story the patron has selected for presentation, but also takes on the responsibility of the arrangement of all the play's subsequent action. He is accompanied by two or three instrumentalists, who play different kinds of drum, the *maddale* and the *chande*, against a harmonium drone that provides a continuous single note. His primary job (all parts in traditional yakshagana are taken by men) is to pick up the thread of the narrative between dances and improvised scenes performed by the actors and keep the performance moving along. The actors may improvise between themselves or with the bhagavata.

146

After the invocation a fool character known as the *Hanu-manyaka* arrives on the stage, and after dialogue with the bhagavata subsequently remains to irreverently quiz the other characters as they arrive. The main characters are introduced with an introductory dance called an *oddolaga* and reveal themselves gradually from behind a curtain (originally known as a *yavanika*) held up by two stage hands, emphasizing the dramatic quality of the revelation. The actors' dancing is often energetic and exuberant, with high leaps and kicks, made even more demanding by the characteristic giant, brightly coloured crown or turban (*mundasu*), an embroidered and ornamented jacket and some nine yards of check-patterned *dhoti* tied around the waist.

It will be helpful to identify those elements from the yaksha-gana tradition that are to be found in Girish Karnad's *Hayavadana*. Chief among these is the Bhagavata, who acts as narrator and sings for and about the characters in both third and first person, often revealing their thoughts, and orchestrating the extemporized dances and prose exchanges of the performers. An intimate relationship through direct contact is established with the audience from the outset, and maintained throughout the performance. In *Hayavadana* the yakshagana tradition is followed in Bhagavata's opening song, providing an invocation to the elephant-headed god Ganesha, the remover of all obstacles to the play's performance. In this context, however, the god has an additional significance that depends on knowing a little of the story of his mythological origins.

Ganesha, it will be remembered, is the child of the goddess Parvati, brought to life from moulded sandalwood paste. Standing guard at the door during his mother's bathing, the determined boy confronts the god Siva, who has returned to visit his wife. Not prepared to let the stranger pass, Ganesha makes a surprisingly robust defence and Siva is obliged to call up armies to engage in battle with this unlikely yet fearsome opponent. Eventually, however, Ganesha loses his head when Siva becomes no longer prepared to tolerate the insolent child's obstruction, uttering a magic mantra to effect the decapitation. However, Siva's troubles are not at an end since Parvati, emerging from her bath, flies into a terrible rage when she discovers what has happened, manifesting herself in all her deadly forms. In desperation Siva instructs one of his soldiers to bring the head of the first living thing he can find and place it on top of the decapitated boy who he will then revive. Lumbering around the corner comes an elephant and before a second thought can be given the deed is done and Parvati's child is restored to life ... with the head of an elephant. Siva's trepidations are assuaged once it becomes clear that his wife is intrigued and delighted with the boy's new form. What more appropriate deity could there be to sanction a play about transposed heads?

In Karnad's play the musicians sit to one side of the stage where they accompany the Bhagavata, while a chorus also sings, though in poetically descriptive evocation of particular moments rather than presaging the narrative's development. Next comes a comic exchange that mirrors the yakshagana character Hanu-manayaka's entrance. This buffoon part is here played by the actor who will later take Devadatta's role. The arrival of the horse-headed Hayavadana is wonderfully theatricalized with the use of the brightly coloured stage curtain, gradually lowered by two stage hands to reveal the actor's full form. Karnad allows Hayavadana a good many contemporary references to political and social issues, which the yakshagana comedians are similarly permitted, though not the heroic characters that come after them. Curtains are employed again for entrances and exits for Kali, and immediately following the Bhaga-vata's announcement of an interval for the audience to ponder the solution to the exchanged-heads riddle, as well as to represent Padmini's self-immolation or sati.

Yet as well as the similarities, there are very significant differences from yakshagana also, most notably in Karnad's use of masks for two of his main characters rather than elaborate make-up, and his inclusion of the dolls of the second act. Masks are worn only by the two friends Kapila (the blacksmith) and Devadatta (the Brahmin), as well, of course, by Hayavadana himself. There is a pragmatic reason for the use of masks for the central duo. In this way the clever device of the exchange of *masks* effects the head swap of the narrative and crucially determines the actors' playing style both before and after this moment. Each actor must embody the change that the head swap brings about, taking on the vocal characteristics of the other actor, as consistent with the new mask, while retaining the original physical mannerisms of fragile intellectual or muscle-bound blacksmith. Each – but particularly the actor playing Kapila – must then gradually 'revert' to the physicality suggested by the mask, therefore adopting the distinctive movement characteristics of the other actor's original performance. This is perhaps more confusing to hear described than to witness in practice, with skilful actors.

The androgynous dolls, brought back from the fair by Deva-datta (the actor wearing Devadatta's mask) for the boy, partly fulfil the Bhagavata's function in the second act in revealing Padmini's suppressed longings for Kapila, but their observations also convey the transformation Devadatta is undergoing as his miraculously muscular body reverts to type:

DOLL II: What happened?
DOLL I: He touched me, and . . .
DOLL II: Yes?
DOLL I: His palms! They were so rough, when he first brought us here. Like a labourer's. But now they are soft – sickly soft – like a young girl's. (*Hayavadana*, p.47)

Girish Karnad has made it clear that the dolls are also intended to fulfil another function:

> I had a definite reason for using them. In the first half, the Devadatta-Kapil[a]-Padmini story goes on without interruptions. Even the Bhagavata sings or comments only where there's no character on the stage. No song interrupts the flow of the story. In the second half the story is continually interrupted by the dolls, the songs and the Bhagavata interferes in the action, talks to the characters, comments on their mental state. This is done merely to bring out the disintegrated state of the three people's lives. In the first half everything is neat and clear, but in the second I wanted to create the impression of a reflection in a broken mirror – all fragmented, repetitious, out-of-focus, all bits and pieces.[5]

---

[5] *Ibid.*, pp. 18–19, letter to Pratibha Agrawal, 5 July 1971.

In many ways, *Hayavadana* is Padmini's story: from her first appearance she is on stage virtually throughout. She also has no mask, implying that our perception of Kapila and Devadatta is to be through her eyes. Padmini is in pursuit of an unattainable ideal in which the respective qualities she esteems in each of her lovers are combined: she wishes to have her cake and eat it. She is certainly manipulative in her treatment of both Kapila (her cross-questioning at their first meeting) and Devadatta (her change of heart over the trip to Ujjain), and her encounter with Kali comically further demonstrates her selfishness:

PADMINI: ... why didn't you stop Devadatta when he came here? Why didn't you stop Kapila? If you'd saved either of them, I would have been spared all this terror, this agony. Why did you wait so long? (*Hayavadana*, p. 32)

Her replacing of the heads on the wrong bodies is completely accidental, as her subsequent reaction to what she has done makes clear, and Kali, resignedly realizing the mistake Padmini has made, decides not to intervene yet again in the foolish mortal's actions ('My dear daughter, there should be a limit even to honesty'), but allows the consequences of the reversal to take their course ('anyway so be it'), and for Padmini, perhaps, to get her just deserts.

Yet the unfolding of the moral is never reduced to simplistic aphorism. There are deeper and more serious issues concerning identity and completeness to emerge even though Karnad suffuses the play with lightness and humour, not least in the reappearance of the now all but complete horse Hayavadana at the play's conclusion, where the main narrative and the framing story merge. The boy, Padmini's son, who survived his mother's fate and has the power to complete himself, the horse and the play, acquires a symbolic role as progenitor of a future generation, yet clinging to his dolls he seems incapable of the simplest kind of social interaction. Hayavadana, almost complete, struggles to lose his 'cursed' human voice by singing the national anthem – which (he has noticed) always seems to ruin people's voices – though without success. Ultimately, the interdependence of these two 'incompletes' is made apparent when the comic spectacle of Hayavadana provokes the boy's socialization, the child now laughing and riding on the horse's back, and the shared laughter turns the horse's human whine into a whinny.

Hayavadana, perhaps, takes on the metaphorical significance of nationhood itself, the unity of which depends not on the empty singing of the words of a national anthem, but on the liberation and integration of a people through laughter and joy in the acceptance of human weakness and incompleteness, and in the celebration of the pairing of horse and rider, nation and people.

It would be impossible to dispute Suresh Awasthi's assertion that in *Hayavadana* Girish Karnad has created one of India's most important contemporary plays (it received the Natya Sangh award for the best play of 1971). The play is rich in its theatrical language drawn in part from folk theatre traditions, complex in its multidimensional thematic aspects of identity, search for ideal, completeness and incompleteness: all rooted in the narrative treasures from India's mythological storehouse. Yet it is also important to acknowledge the playwright's desire to use folk traditions only insofar as they serve his purpose in structuring the form of his play. Karnad has explained that even though he had to 'grope [his] way to find the final form of *Hayavadana*' it was with the conviction that the use of traditional forms had no need to coincide with the propagation of traditional values: 'The energy of the folk theatre comes from the fact that while it seems to support traditional values, it is also capable of subverting them, looking at them from various points of view. . . . The form can give rise to a genuine dialectic.'[6]

Karnad's theatre-writing career has been frequently interrupted by other activities, including many contributions to cinema and television, as screenwriter, director and performer. In fact his popular reputation in India perhaps rests more on his acting appearances in television dramas than it does on playwriting. The consequences for Girish Karnad, and those like him who have confronted the necessity of making a living outside theatre, have been firstly that his stage plays have been written rather sporadically over the years and that, secondly, he has felt to some extent responsible for

---

[6] Karnad, 'Theatre in India', p. 347.

perpetuating the amateurism of the medium to which he would prefer to devote himself:

> The major concern of the Indian theatre in the post-
> Independence period has been to try to define its 'Indianness'
> and to relate itself to the past from which it was cut off. The
> awful part is that most of these explorations have been done by
> enthusiastic amateurs, who find it extremely difficult to
> continue to work in theatre. Most of them have to go into film
> or television, thus perpetuating the amateur status of the
> theatre they have helped to keep alive. I see myself as a
> playwright, but I make a living in film and television. There is
> a very high elasticity of substitution between the different
> performing media in India: the participant gets tossed about
> violently.[7]

It is evident from these remarks that Girish Karnad sees the direction of progress in contemporary Indian theatre along the same lines as Awasthi's 'return to and discovery of tradition ... inspired by a search for roots and a quest for identity'. Though experienced from the point of view of his own playwriting, for Karnad this process has, to some extent, been compromised by the exigencies of ensuring financial security through working in media that, while rewarding in their own ways, do not permit the same kind of explorations that theatre makes possible by virtue of the traditions it may tap.

Just prior to Girish Karnad's appointment as chair of the Sangeet Natak Akademi at New Delhi in 1988, he had spent a year in the United States as Fulbright scholar in residence at the Department of South Asian Languages and Civilizations at the University of Chicago. Here he was able to study the *Natyasastra* in detail, clarifying his thoughts about classical Indian theatre in the preparation of taught courses for students at the university, and make a return to playwriting after a lengthy absence.

The *Natyasastra* is traditionally credited with a holy origin, arising from Lord Brahma's collation of elements from the four ancient Vedas, or collections of the sacred hymns of Hinduism. How-

---

[7] *Ibid.*, pp. 348–9.

ever, it is dated much later than the Vedas, at between 200 BC and 200 AD. It contains some 5,500 verses on every facet of performance: acting, playwriting and production. Sometimes compared with Aristotle's *Poetics*, its authorship has been attributed to the sage Bharata, who may have been a Brahmin priest. Though the discussion of dramatic form in the *Natyasastra* is certainly not categorized into tragedy, comedy and epic, Bharata's explanation of the concept of rasa (the eight basic human sentiments being identified as eroticism, humour, pathos, anger, valour, terror, disgust and wonder) indicates a comparable interest in the nature of audience response to the drama, an interest that goes far beyond Aristotle in its prescriptive detail. The systematic codification of a physical language of performance that the *Natyasastra* contains is clearly beyond the scope of any description here, suffice it to say that the actor-dancer's body is divided into major and minor parts with every nuance of facial, gestural and vocal expression set out.

In relation to Girish Karnad's work, it is important to consider the prominence given by Bharata in the *Natyasastra* to the role played by the *sutradhara*. Though commonly translated as 'stage manager', the sutradhara fulfilled a very different role from that conjured up by a contemporary understanding of this title. The sutradhara means literally the 'string holder', translated as 'puppet master' or 'manipulator', though he was almost certainly an actor himself and played not merely an impresario's role. He predates the bhagavath of yakshagana, with whom he bears many similarities, as controller of the stage action, orchestrator of the musicians, director and choreographer of the actor-dancers and, fundamentally, during the performance itself, storyteller. In many ways the sutradhara is 'the story' itself. As well as the storyteller, it is also important to remember the prevalence of stock characters in Sanskrit drama, to which the *Natyasastra* refers, like the king, queen, bride, bridegroom, sage, wise woman, clown and villain. Such characters appear frequently in Karnad's plays.

Karnad's contact with his friend, distinguished Indian folklore and culture scholar, Professor A. K. Ramanujan at the University of Chicago prompted a renewed interest in finding a dramatic form for the treatment of two Karnatak folk-tales Ramanujan had introduced him to, and which he was eventually to work into *Nāga-Mandala* (*Play with a Cobra*, 1990). A production of the play, translated into English by Karnad himself, was performed at the University Theater at Chicago and subsequently at the Guthrie Theater in Minneapolis.

Nāga-Mandala inventively harnesses the intensity of the imaginative experience that the Indic oral tradition allows, through the economy of its dramatic structure and its theatrical simplicity. As with *Hayavadana*, the main action of the play is framed at beginning and end, this time with the writer himself participating in the creative process and drawing the audience's attention to the evolutionary nature and self-conscious theatricality of the journey all the participants find themselves on. The beautifully crafted prologue is important in establishing the style of the presentation, as well as bringing out the motif of domestic relationships that is present throughout. Structurally, the inclusion of a prologue also interestingly echoes both folk and classical Indian performance traditions.

It is night and the audience is instantly engaged by the lone figure of a man seated in the moonlight in the inner sanctum of a ruined temple. He declares himself to be a playwright, and explains that he may die unless he can stay awake through the whole night, having been cursed by a mendicant as a result of making so many of his audiences soporific in the past. Vowing to 'abjure all story-telling, all play-acting' if his wish is vouchsafed, his witty opening is interrupted by the fluttering arrival of the gossiping lamp flames, on whom the man eavesdrops from the shadows, animatedly giggling and chattering about their respective releases from service in the home. The kerosene flame's story will convey the idea:

FLAME 4: My master had an old, ailing mother. Her stomach was bloated, her back covered with bed sores. The house stank of cough and phlegm, pus and urine. No one got a wink of sleep at night. Naturally, I stayed back too. The old lady died this morning, leaving behind my master and his young wife, young and juicy as a tender cucumber. I was chased out fast. (*Nāga-Mandala*, p. 3)

The Story, in the form of a woman dressed in a colourful sari, walks on to the stage following the last flame's tale, seamlessly connecting New Flame's oral description with a dramatic representation and, once the Flames have settled down following their startled disturbance by the Man's interruption from his hiding place to plead to be the Story's listener (it will help keep him awake), the prologue is over and the musicians are called for Rani's story to begin.

Like so many village folk-tales the central story of *Nāga-Mandala* is a simple one, though, rather like a kaleidoscope, on each re-examination the patterns of emphasis shift and new meanings emerge. There are many stories about new brides and grooms in India, and this adaptation of one from Karnataka emphasizes the cementing of the marriage union through the discovery and awakening of sexuality, primarily from a woman's point of view.

Rani is newly married and kept a prisoner under lock and key at home in the village by a possessive, suspicious, yet brutally uncaring husband who returns each day merely to demand the midday meal she is instructed to cook for him. Appanna (which means 'any man'), exerts a remorselessly authoritarian regime over his wife and shows her no affection: his sexual energies are directed elsewhere. An old blind woman, transported everywhere on her son's back, takes pity on the girl and passes through the window's bars a magic aphrodisiac root, which, she believes, will instantly 'make her a wife' (thus solving all her problems), once it is mixed with her husband's food. The first (small) root fails to take effect: the second (large) root causes the curry into which it has been placed to explode in such a steaming red froth that, in a panic, Rani tips the contents of the pot into an ant-hill beside the house. There, the potion's power takes effect on a king-cobra who, disguising himself in human form as Appanna, now visits Rani nightly, slithering through a drain that serves the house. In spite of her bewilderment at the contradictions between her husband's daytime attitude and night-time behaviour, gradually she warms to his after-dark affections and begins to long for his visits. Matters come to a head when Appanna accuses his wife, now several months pregnant, of infidelity and, facing the judgement of the village elders on the matter, Rani is forced to undergo a trial by ordeal. Under the cobra's prior instruction, she elects to place her hand in the ant-hill and withdraw the king-cobra. The village is astonished by Rani's feat and deify her, the elders instructing Appanna to honour her divinity. Appanna asks for his wife's forgiveness, his concubine becomes the family's servant and a beautiful child is born to the couple.

The story form gives Girish Karnad not only the opportunity to include folk elements of music, song and dance within the play, but also to convey a sense of spontaneous storytelling through the characters' willingness to interrupt their progress to refer back to the teller before proceeding. For example, grinding the large root for preparation in the curry, Rani asks the Story, 'Shall I pour it in?', to which the Story, following the sutradhara convention of the *Natya-sastra* in directing the play's action, replies in the affirmative. The stage spectators gathered around the acting area reinforce the notion of a story being told in the here and now, and are also active participants in the play: the Flames surrounding Rani and Naga (the name given to her cobra husband) join together in a dance and song in celebration of their union. In true epic style, and confirming Karnad's central interest in narratology within the play, the Man also intervenes to have the Story and the actors rework the ending of the play as an epilogue to 'happy ever after' three times in three different ways. What about Rani's discovery when her husband climbed into bed with her that he is someone new? What about her anguish at the loss of her lover?

STORY: When one says, 'And they lived happily ever after', all that is taken for granted. You sweep such headaches under the pillow and then press your head firmly down on them. (*Nāga-Mandala*, p. 41)

But the cobra is not to be forgotten. In the next ending Naga's love is his death, as he curls himself in the tresses of Rani's hair as she lies sleeping with her husband and child, only to be combed out dead when she wakes. Knowingly, she asks Appanna that their son should perform the cremation ritual for the snake and commemorate his death annually. But this proves too unhappy an ending for the Flames. At last, *Nāga-Mandala* finds its completion as the tiny cobra takes its refuge in Rani's hair with her consent, now secret symbol of her wedded bliss. The night, with the story, is over.

The simplicity of the staging is essential to the theatrical adaptation of the narrative. Almost everything can be mimed (locks, doors, windows, boiling pots, barking dogs, glasses of milk) by the actors, though Karnad prefers the use of a puppet cobra operated by a performer in blacks. Lighting changes economically shift the scene from night- to daytime, with the actors' help:

NAGA: It's almost morning. I must go.

RANI: (*waking up*) What?

NAGA: I have to go.

RANI: (*gently*) Go.

> (*She turns away.* NAGA *takes a step to go. They both freeze.*
> *The lights change sharply from night to mid-day. In a flash,*
> NAGA *becomes* APPANNA: *Pushes her to the floor and kicks her.*)

APPANNA: Aren't you ashamed to admit it, you harlot? I locked you in, and yet you managed to find a lover! Tell me who it is. Who did you go to with your sari off? (*Nāga-Mandala*, p. 33)

Yet technology is not always needed for Girish Karnad skilfully to make the dramatic form (always in danger of revealing its limitations against the flexibility of its narrative counterpart) work to advantage, as when the elders of the village meet for Rani's ordeal:

ELDER III: But you insist on swearing by the King Cobra. The news has spread and, as you can see, attracted large crowds. (*Nāga-Mandala*, p. 36)

Here, all of the audience is included in the 'large crowds'.

It is a pity that there is insufficient room in the play for a fuller development of the secondary story of Kurudavva (the blind woman) and her son Kappanna, since the new bride's experience of the loss of her parents as she gains a husband is very cleverly juxtaposed with a (sightless) mother's loss of her son as he reaches sexual maturity. Kappanna's transfixing visions of a friendly, but apparently predatory, female spirit are precursors of his subsequent abduction by a ghostly woman, as described by his now desolate and inconsolable mother. Kappanna has proven to be the comic muff of the first act, and Kurudavva's explanation of his departure in the second is as humorous as it is salacious:

KURUDAVVA: I woke up. It was midnight. I heard him panting. He was not in his bed. He was standing up ... stiff ... like a wooden pillar.

Suddenly I knew. There was someone else in the house. A third
person. . . . What woman would come inside our house at that hour?
And how? She wasn't even breathing. I shouted: 'Who are you? What
do you want from us? Go away!' Suddenly the door burst open. The
rushing wind shook the rafters. He slipped from my hands and was
gone. Never came back. (*Nāga-Mandala*, p.38)

The sexual imagery in *Nāga-Mandala* is obvious, though its
interpretation is open to question. Rani endures physical imprisonment and mental anguish, if not a kind of psychological torture, in
her totally different experiences of her two husbands, by day and by
night, compounded by the fact that she is sworn by the cobra never to
question this paradoxical dualism. Her ultimate deification by the
Elders after trial by ordeal (rather similar to the kind undergone by so-
called witches of Tudor England):

ELDER I: Appanna, your wife is not an ordinary woman. She is a
goddess incarnate. Don't grieve that you judged her wrongly and
treated her badly.

seems to excuse 'any man's' appalling ill-treatment of any 'ordinary
woman'.

Yet it is true that Rani is also both sexually naive and prudish.
When Kurudavva explains that on eating the root Appanna will 'make
you a wife instantly', Rani replies, 'But I am his wife already.' When
Naga's show of affection brings her to embrace him, she suddenly
breaks away after his kiss and, crying, accuses him of being a 'bad
man' who she would never have agreed to marry if she had known
that he had such intentions. He gently explains the inexorable sexual
energies of the natural world:

NAGA: Frogs croaking in pelting rain, tortoises singing soundlessly in
the dark, foxes, crabs, ants, rattlers, sharks, swallows – even the geese!
The female begins to smell like the wet earth. And stung by her smell,
the King Cobra starts searching for his Queen. The tiger bellows for his
mate. When the flame-of-forest blossoms into a fountain of red and the
earth cracks open at the touch of the aerial roots of the banyan, it
moves in the hollow of the cottonwood, in the flow of the estuary, the
dark limestone caves from the womb of the heavens to the dark

netherworlds, within everything that sprouts, grows, stretches, creaks and blooms – everywhere, those who come together, cling, fall apart lazily! It is there and there and there, everywhere. (*Nāga-Mandala*, p. 25)

From the moment Rani glimpses Naga's reflection as the cobra in her mirror-box, the ambiguity of her subsequent knowledge and understanding of her night visitor is established. The play's final ending, as the tiny cobra slithers secretly into the tresses of her hair, might be seen as representative of Rani's discovery, acceptance and 'ownership' of her own sexual pleasure, crucial to her independence and emotional wellbeing.

Girish Karnad's loyalty to an oral and written language, enriched by the folkloric and mythic bedrock that has helped shape it, in combination with his passion for exploring the performance languages offered by classical and folk traditions, have placed him among the front-runners in the 'return to roots' movement of contemporary Indian theatre practitioners.

Yet Karnad, in many ways, fits uneasily into this category to which he may be assigned by virtue of the particular forms and themes of the relatively few plays he has written for the theatre over the years. His recent play, called *Talé-daṇḍa* (1993), is acknowledged to have been written partly in response to intercommunal violence, exemplified by the Hindu–Muslim confrontation over the temple site at Ayodhya. Yet like *Tughlaq*, it has an historical rather than a contemporary setting, tracing the story of the twelfth-century poet-saint Basavanna and his followers who sought, unsuccessfully, to demolish caste barriers.

Though preoccupied with history and myth, Karnad is certainly no romantic idealist. Saddled with being perceived as the playwright of traditional folk forms, Karnad declared 'If I see another Ganesh, I'll scream' in an interview following the completion of *Talé-daṇḍa*.[8] Girish Karnad might well concur with K. S. Kothari's view that the post-independence quest in Indian theatre has been for 'that indefinable quality called "Indianness"', but not only

---

[8] Interview with Madhu Jain in *India Today*, 15 March 1992, pp. 68–9.

is such a quality *indefinable*, like India herself, the very concept of an 'Indian' theatre is an abstraction, an impossible convergence of manifestly diverse practices and traditions that collectively and conveniently gathered into a single concept can only possibly have relevance to 'foreign' theatre.

Perhaps the point is that Karnad's pragmatism always prevails: that the reason for writing is just as important as the means of the theme's expression. History and myth provide simultaneous visions of the world, equally complex in their relationship with present experience. The prevalence of kings and kingdoms in the plays (King Yayati, Sultan Muhammad, King Dharmasheela, King Cobra, King Bijda) indicates the centrality of responsibility in the exercise of power between rulers and ruled, responsibility on both sides, and in all its forms.

Conclusion

Though the dramatists discussed here write from and of a common condition of cultural subordination and oppression, and share the desire to use the theatre to explore and affirm their cultural substance, it must by now be evident that they have done so in remarkably diverse ways. This has to do, inevitably, both with differing personal imaginative orientations and with the particular cultural realities that have nourished them. For example, the nature of colonialism in western Nigeria was such that traditional ritual belief and practice have remained as an everyday reality and as a rich and immediate source for Soyinka's dramatic imagination. But for dramatists of the black diaspora, such as Derek Walcott and August Wilson, the link with their cultural heritage is more problematic and requires a greater effort of reclamation. The need to restore that heritage – and to restore it as a vital part of the contemporary self – are crucial themes of their writing, as they are not in Soyinka, even while they both make powerful metaphorical and formal use of features of their popular cultural traditions, through folklore and blues music respectively. For Jack Davis, on the other hand, since the focus is very much on the struggle to resist immediate injustice and to assert the fundamental human and political rights of Aborigines, the evocation of the heritage is much more subdued, and much more elegiac in mood.

These and other differences are sufficiently evident from the preceding chapters not to need elaborately spelling out here. What is perhaps more interesting and important, looking at this dramatic writing as a whole, is not inevitable difference but certain underlying affinities between the dramatists, even when the surface features are sometimes quite dissimilar. One such affinity, which seems particularly prominent and important, is the special significance attached to myth and the mythic in playwrights otherwise as distinctive as Soyinka, Walcott, Karnad and Wilson.

The 'return to roots', in search of a fully restored cultural identity and self-confidence, often seems to involve a mode of thought and being, invoked and explored by several of our dramatists, that is quite alien to the settled habits of Western rationalism and its customary assumptions about history. Towards the end of his remarkable extended reflection on Mexican and Latin American history and culture, *The Labyrinth of Solitude*, Octavio Paz comments on the opposition between history and myth in terms of their different conceptions of time. In its mythic form, time is 'not succession and transition', but rather 'the perpetual source of a fixed present' in which all times, past and future, are contained. It is, according to Paz, 'impregnated with all the particulars of our lives: it is as long as eternity or as short as a breath', and it is marked by 'an indivisible unity' between itself and life. Chronometric time, the time of history, on the other hand, 'is not an immediate apprehension of the flow of reality but is instead a rationalization of its passing', in which we become the prisoners of the clock and the calendar. In Paz's imagining, we were at some point exiled from 'the centre of the world', that eternity in which all times were one, and forced to enter the time of history. But we are still able to emerge, occasionally, from the solitude of historical time into the 'communion' of mythic time – through fiestas and religious ritual, through folk- and fairytales, poetry and theatrical performance. In such special events, says Paz, 'mythical time – father of all the times that mask reality – coincides with our inner, subjective time':

> Man, the prisoner of succession, breaks out of his invisible jail
> and enters living time: his subjective life becomes identical
> with exterior time, because this has ceased to be a spatial
> measurement and has changed into a source, a spring, in the
> absolute present, endlessly re-creating itself.[1]

[1] Octavio Paz, *The Labyrinth of Solitude*, Harmondsworth: Penguin, 1985, p.198.

Something akin to Paz's conception of mythic time is evident in Soyinka's discussion of time in the Yoruba world view in *Myth, Literature and the African World*:

> The Yoruba is not, like European man, concerned with the purely conceptual aspects of time; they are too concretely realised in his own life, religion, sensitivity, to be mere tags for explaining the metaphysical order of his world. If we may put the same thing in fleshed-out cognitions, life, present life, contains within it manifestations of the ancestral, the living and the unborn.[2]

As in Paz, this is a notion of time associated with a myth of primal, undifferentiated being which was destroyed by a Luciferian act of rebellion against the supreme Yoruba deity Orisanla, and then partially repaired, subsequently, by the heroic feat of Ogun in bridging the gulf of transition. Like Paz's fiestas and religious rituals, the ritual drama of the Yoruba permits the participant to 'indulge in symbolic transactions to recover his totality of being', disquieted as he is by his memory of the 'primal severance' and his loss of 'the eternal essence of his being'.[3]

Something of this mythic conception of time and being is also dramatized in August Wilson's work, especially in the form of Bynum's 'song' and the visionary experience with the 'shiny man' that first introduced him to it. It is also present in the epic and folkloric underpinnings of Girish Karnad's theatre, which go beyond formal and narrative borrowings into participation, however critical and contemporary, in a 'mythic' sense of life. And though, as we've seen, Jack Davis has concentrated his attention on the urgent realities of contemporary urban Aboriginal life, his drama is always underlaid by a sense of the traditional culture that for many Aborigines has been all but lost, with its profoundly mythic understanding of the 'dreaming' and of the roots of our human existence.

There is nothing particularly mysterious about this. The cultures to which these dramatists belong, and about and for which

[2] Wole Soyinka, *Myth, Literature and the African World*, p. 144.
[3] *Ibid.*, p. 144.

they write, have retained, often as the basis of their world views, a 'pre-industrial' understanding of reality which is intrinsically spirit-ual and mythic. Seeking to make sense of contemporary, often deeply alienated experience, and to reaffirm their people's cultural person-ality, writers naturally explore not just particular myths from their cultures but the pervading sense of the mythic, as the expression of an organic and integrated existence, which is so often their heritage. Nor is it surprising if their explorations vary widely, depending on the historical contexts in which they write, as well as personal creative factors. If August Wilson's preoccupation with the non-rational, spiritual force embodied in the 'song' serves the fundamental aim of returning black Americans to their African roots and what the playwright seems to regard as their primal African personality, it is a quite different matter for the African Soyinka, whose exploitation of a mythic understanding of reality seems to be primarily linked in his drama to his preoccupation with the exercise of power in post-independence Africa. A sense of the mythic, in short, may be associated with varying political agendas.

And, of course, the political and historical preoccupations of a playwright in a subordinated culture may be devoid of, or at least subdue, the sense of the mythic as described by Paz, Soyinka and others. This is certainly the case with Badal Sircar and with the 'workshop' plays of Fugard, Kani and Ntshona, or with a later example of the genre such as *Woza Albert!* – though even here the myth of the resurrection has a crucial dramatic function. In these plays the immediate problems of political and social oppression are at the forefront of dramatic attention, more or less to the exclusion of the ritualistic and mythic dimension of life explored in plays like *A Dance of the Forests*, *Joe Turner's Come and Gone* or *Dream on Monkey Mountain*. But it is interesting and surely significant that even with such politically radical writers as the black American Amiri Baraka (LeRoi Jones) and the Kenyan Ngugi wa Thiong'o – to extend our range beyond dramatists considered here – their polemical and revolutionary theatre seeks an experience of 'communion' for all the participants. In such a conception the theatre becomes an arena of expanding communal consciousness, and the images and impact of the stage presentation tend naturally towards the 'mythic'.

For example, in Ngugi's *The Trial of Dedan Kimathi*, co-written with Micere Githae Mugo, the audience is offered a fervent protest against neo-colonialism in Kenya, and a call to renew the struggle, which Dedan Kimathi is seen as having heroically served, for genuine national liberation. Though a genuinely historical figure – Kimathi was a Mau Mau guerrilla leader in the struggle against the British – he is invested throughout the play with a 'mythic' quality and is presented as a redemptive epic hero whose heroic struggle against evil, whose temptations, betrayal, trial and condemnation all parallel the life and sufferings of Christ. Kimathi performs miracles, metaphorically if not quite literally, on behalf of the Kenyan masses. Faith in his cause can achieve the apparently impossible. A character makes an explicit connection between the Christian call and the 'call of our people'; and Kimathi implicitly likens himself to the Saviour when he accuses his betrayers of being 'Judases' who have deserted him for thirty pieces of silver. During his 'temptations' and trial, he is forced to undergo the same humiliations as Christ, and similar attempts to divert him from his redemptive function. The breaking of the loaf of bread in the courtroom to reveal the instrument of redemption, the gun, is an evident allusion to Christian symbolism, and a striking transference of its redemptive theology to the secular, revolutionary arena. And the mythic connotations of Dedan Kimathi's presentation as a martyred redeemer are reinforced by the dramatists' handling of time, 'so that past and future and present flow into one another' (production note), and their framing of the play by tableaux that enact the oppressed history and ultimate triumph of black people.

The Trial of Dedan Kimathi seems to conform to Amiri Baraka's fiercely polemical prescription for the 'Revolutionary Theatre' not only in its political aims, but also in the way it 'take[s] dreams and give[s] them a reality' and 'isolate[s] the ritual and historical cycles of reality'.[4] Though Octavio Paz makes an opposition between history and myth and their different perceptions of

---

[4] See Amiri Baraka, 'The Revolutionary Theatre' in *Home, Social Essays*, anthologized in *Selected Plays and Prose of Amiri Baraka/ LeRoi Jones*, New York: Morrow, 1979, pp. 130–3.

time, history itself tends to be perceived here as a mythic or ritualized drama, as it is in Amiri Baraka's own theatre. And it suggests that, whatever their particular politics or ideological orientations, for dramatists writing from a pervasive sense of oppression the shaping of their material in mythic and ritualistic forms is a congenial element in their expression of cultural identity.

Even the youngest of the dramatists considered here are old enough to belong to a generation that achieved its artistic maturity in the first decades after national independence or, in, in the cases of Davis, Wilson and Fugard, to a generation that fought for and won substantial gains in human and political rights. But in the last decade of the century those struggles and victories are increasingly distant historical prospects, in some respects now remote from contemporary realities and concerns. Also, all the dramatists discussed are men. And this is not because of authorial male chauvinism, or ignorance of the fact that women dramatists have contributed to the cultures with which this book is concerned, but because there is simply no female dramatist, in this context, of a recognizably similar status to the male playwrights treated here. (Or, for that matter, of comparable status to women novelists such as Bessy Head, Nadine Gordimer, Toni Morrison and a good many others.) Some of our playwrights have written extensively and with insight about women's experience – notably Jack Davis, who gives particular prominence in his work to the crucial role played by women in the 'crisis' of the urban Aboriginal family. Others have either relegated female experience to the margins of their drama, or – and Soyinka is the main case in point – have arguably adopted conservative, even reactionary, attitudes to women in their plays. In any case, the condition of women as the most oppressed of the oppressed has received much less attention in published post-colonial drama than it should have done.

If we were judging by the numbers of plays by women published internationally, we would have to conclude that female playwrights are still seriously under-represented in the post-colonial context. But we must be careful not to equate the health of the theatre with the availability of published play texts. If there has been no breakthrough by women dramatists in Africa or India to compare with the striking emergence of women writers in much Western theatre, or with female prose writers, there has nevertheless been an encouraging growth in theatre reflecting indigenous feminist 'movements'. It is difficult, internationally, to find published material by or about them, but we should at least be aware of the remarkable work achieved by such groups as the women's theatre collective Sistren in Jamaica, by playwrights such as Mahasweta Devi and Dolly Mehta in India, and by workshopped productions such as *You Strike the Woman, You Strike the Rock* in South Africa.

The same point applies more generally to recent theatre in 'post-colonial' contexts. The range and interest of the work currently being performed in much of the Third World and among subordinated communities in countries like South Africa, Australia and America is not reflected in the availability of texts internationally. Some of this is 'conventional' in the sense that it is the product of a single writer, which is then performed in an urban theatre, usually for an educated, middle-class audience. But some of the most stimulating theatre currently being performed breaks this mould and represents a variety of attempts to depart from metropolitan models to create performance specifically addressing local realities for local audiences. By its very nature this is work that is unlikely to reach or even be of much interest to a larger international audience. Written down (probably having had to be translated from an indigenous language), it may not appear to be of great artistic merit, compared with the literary mastery of a Soyinka or a Walcott. But seen on a stage (often of an impromptu kind) and witnessed by its appropriate audience, such theatre may be remarkably powerful in its impact and exciting in its use of a variety of indigenous performance models, such as storytelling, dance, mime, puppetry and so forth. While such drama may be the product of a single writer, it is often collectively devised and highly improvisational in form, sometimes involving members of local communities in its creation or even performance. Examples range from the 'Theatre of the Oppressed' of Augusto Boal and other practitioners in Latin America, to the pioneering work of PETA (the Philippines Educational Theatre Association), the 'Theatre for Development' movement in Africa, and community projects involving theatre such as the Kamiriithu Community Education and Cultural

Centre in Limuru, established by Ngugi wa Thiong'o and his associates before their arrest and subsequent exile from Kenya.

Nevertheless, theatre in these cultures faces many of the difficulties familiar to theatre practitioners in the West, only on a much greater scale. The main problem is almost always financial – a basic lack of resources. And just as theatre in the West has had to face the challenge of rival media such as film, television and video, so too does theatre in the Third World. In spite of the healthy profusion of theatrical experiments, many of them community-based, exploring and representing contemporary post-colonial experience, it is a fact that, as in the West, some of the brightest young talents have too often not chosen the theatre as their favoured medium of expression. The 'mainstream' theatre, in many countries, is therefore weaker than it should be, not only in the absence of writers but also of performers, directors and designers, who can earn better incomes and often gain more professional satisfaction elsewhere.

One of the main arguments structuring Edward Said's magisterial *Culture and Imperialism* is that the historical experience of imperialism brought about an extraordinarily complex fusion of interconnected experience between cultures at every level while, paradoxically, allowing people to believe 'that they were only mainly, exclusively, white, black, or Western, or Oriental'.[5] For Said, the task now is to transcend static notions of identity and the orthodox insistence on the separation of cultures, and to explore and affirm 'the interdependence of various histories *on* one another, and the necessary interaction of contemporary societies *with* one another'.[6] Through this 'contrapuntal' approach it becomes possible not only to achieve a fuller understanding of the experience of the subjugated, but to come to terms with the often hidden but nevertheless crucial basis of so much of our own modern culture, and its literature and thought. Perhaps most importantly, we may be enabled to see how what we have come to accept, unquestioningly, as 'our' identity, 'our' tradition, 'our' cultural essence have in reality been formed through

[5] Edward Said, *Culture and Imperialism*, p. 408.
[6] *Ibid.*, p. 43

interaction with others, since 'it is the case that no identity can ever exist by itself and without an array of opposites, negatives, opposi-tions'.[7]

Though Said himself is primarily interested in literary rather than theatrical texts his fundamental argument applies as much to the drama as to prose fiction. The dramatists we have considered, as well as others whose work we have not been able to discuss, tell something of the other narratives, the other histories that we have largely ignored in the dominating cultures. But they also tell us, in ways that we have not yet perhaps fully appreciated, about ourselves, our own histories and discourses. One instance of how this may happen is the light that a reading of writers such as Fanon, Walcott or Soyinka may throw on a playwright that we normally think of as one of 'ours'. Brian Friel has been preoccupied in many of his plays with themes that we have seen recurring in these pages: the relationship of language and power (the renaming of the Irish countryside in *Translations*), the struggle to find a voice to articulate one's experi-ence (again, in *Translations*, embodied in the character of Sarah), the sense of being a victim of a history determined from 'outside', the continuing if usually repressed power of the ritualistic and mythic (memorably evoked in the dancing scene of *Dancing at Lughnasa*), the introspective concern with the nature and function of art and the artist in a subordinated society (expressed metaphorically through Frank in *Faith Healer*).

Friel's drama shares these concerns with African and Carib-bean and black American playwrights because he has emerged from, and writes about, a common colonial and neo-colonial context, even if in this case it is on our own doorstep. Is it fanciful, then to read the undisputed masterpiece of another Irishman – in fact the undisputed masterpiece of postwar Western drama – in the light this generated? If it is, the temptation is at least understandable, since *Waiting for Godot* is about two characters at the margin of history and society, who have apparently lost all power of self-determination and await a redemption that therefore never comes; and two other characters, the master and the slave, joined by their rope, one voluble but saying

---

[7] *Ibid.*, p. 60.

nothing, the other struggling and failing to give coherent utterance to his thoughts. It may be that such a perspective can be profitably applied to a wide range of theatre, some of it least expected to figure in such a context. And as we, in the current and former centres of empire, expand our ability to think, as Said puts it, 'contrapuntally', with a simultaneous awareness of our own history and of others with which we have been long and formatively intertwined, we shall come to enrich our understanding of our own theatre and culture as well as those of the people we have dominated.

Further reading list

Preface, introduction and conclusion

The following books and articles, which deal more generally with the nature of post-colonial culture and writing, are referred to or are relevant to the discussions in the preface, introduction and conclusion:

Ashcroft, Bill, Griffiths, G. and Tiffin, H., *The Empire Writes Back: Theory and Practice in Post-Colonial Literatures*, London: Routledge, 1989.

Baldwin, James, *The Fire Next Time*, London: Penguin, 1964.

Baraka, Amiri, *Selected Plays and Prose of Amiri Baraka/LeRoi Jones*, New York: Morrow, 1979.

Bharucha, Rustom, *Theatre and the World*, New Delhi: Manohar, 1990.

Fanon, F., *The Wretched of the Earth*, Harmondsworth: Penguin, 1967.
A Dying Colonialism, Harmondsworth: Penguin, 1970.
Black Skin, White Masks, London: Pluto Press, 1986.

King, Bruce, ed., *Post-Colonial English Drama: Commonwealth Drama Since 1960*, New York: St Martin's Press, 1992.

Ngugi wa Thiong'o, *Writers in Politics*, London: Heinemann, 1981.
Barrel of a Pen, London: New Beacon Books, 1983.
Moving the Centre, London: James Currey, 1993.

Paz, Octavio, *The Labyrinth of Solitude*, Harmondsworth: Penguin, 1985.

Said, Edward, W., *Culture and Imperialism*, London: Chatto & Windus, 1993.
'Yeats and Decolonization' in *Literature in the Modern World*, ed. Dennis Walder, Oxford: Oxford University Press, 1990.

Soyinka, Wole, *Myth, Literature and the African World*, Cambridge: Cambridge University Press, 1976.

    Art, Dialogue and Outrage: Essays on Literature and Culture, London: Methuen, 1993.

Derek Walcott and a Caribbean theatre of revelation

Primary sources

The Joker of Seville and O Babylon!, London: Cape, 1979.

Remembrance and Pantomime, New York: Farrar, Straus & Giroux, 1980.

Dream on Monkey Mountain and Other Plays (also contains *The Sea at Dauphin, Ti-Jean and His Brothers, Malcochon, or The Six in the Rain*), New York: Farrar, Straus & Giroux, 1986.

Three Plays (contains *The Last Carnival, Beef, No Chicken, A Branch of the Blue Nile*), New York: Farrar, Straus & Giroux, 1986.

Other criticism

Dabydeen, D., and Wilson-Tagoe, N., *A Reader's Guide to West Indian and Black British Literature*, London: Hamsib Publishing, 1988.

Frickey, P. M., 'Jamaica and Trinidad' in Bruce King, ed., *Post-Colonial English Drama: Commonwealth Drama Since 1960*, New York: St Martin's Press, 1992.

Hill, E., *The Jamaican Stage, 1655–1900*, Amherst: University of Massachusetts Press, 1992.

Juneja, R., 'Derek Walcott' in Bruce King, ed., *Post-Colonial English Drama*.

Naipaul, V. S., *The Middle Passage*, London: Deutsch, 1962.

Omotoso, K., *The Theatrical Into Theatre*, London: New Beacon Books, 1982.

August Wilson's theatre of the blues

Primary sources

Fences and Ma Rainey's Black Bottom, London: Penguin, 1988.

Joe Turner's Come and Gone, New York: Plume, 1988.

The Piano Lesson, New York: Plume, 1990.

Further reading list

Other criticism

Baraka, I. A., *Selected Plays and Prose of Amiri Baraka/LeRoi Jones*, New York: Morrow, 1979.

Fabré, G., *Drumbeats, Masks and Metaphor*, Cambridge, Mass.: Harvard University Press, 1983.

Hill, E., ed., *The Theatre of Black Americans*, New York: Applause Theatre Book Publishers, 1987.

Hill, H., 'Black Theatre into the Mainstream' in Bruce King, ed., *Contemporary American Theatre*, Basingstoke: Macmillan, 1991.

Jack Davis and the drama of Aboriginal history

Primary sources

The main publisher of Australian plays, including those of Jack Davis, is Currency Press in Sydney.

Kullark and The Dreamers, Sydney: Currency Press, 1982.
No Sugar, Sydney: Currency Press, 1986.
Barungin, 1988.

See also

Brisbane, K., ed., *Australia Plays: New Australian Drama* (containing David Williamson, *Travelling North*, Louis Nowra, *The Golden Age*, Jack Davis, *No Sugar*, Michael Gow, *Away*, and Alma De Groen, *The Rivers of China*), London: Nick Hern Books, 1989.

Saunders, J., ed., *Plays From Black Australia* (containing Jack Davis, *The Dreamers*, Eva Johnson, *Murras*, Richard Walley, *Coordah*, and Bob Maza, *The Keepers*), Sydney: Currency Press, 1989.

Other criticism

Davis, J., and Chesson, K., *Jack Davis: a Life-Story*, Melbourne: Dent, 1988.

Holloway, P., ed., *Contemporary Australian Drama: Perspectives Since 1955*, Sydney: Currency Press, 1987.

Kelly, V., 'Louis Nowra' in Bruce King, ed., *Post-Colonial English*

Drama: Commonwealth Drama Since 1960, New York: St
  Martin's Press, 1992.
Williams, M., 'Australia', in Bruce King, ed., *Post-Colonial English
  Drama*.

Wole Soyinka and the Nigerian theatre of ritual vision

Primary sources

Collected Plays 1 (containing *A Dance of the Forests, The Swamp
  Dwellers, The Strong Breed, The Road, The Bacchae of
  Euripides*), London: Oxford University Press, 1973.
Collected Plays 2 (containing *The Lion and the Jewel, Kongi's Harvest,
  The Trials of Brother Jero, Jero's Metamorphosis, Madmen and
  Specialists*), London: Oxford University Press, 1974.
Six Plays (containing *The Trials of Brother Jero, Jero's Metamorphosis,
  Camwood on the Leaves, Death and the King's Horseman,
  Madmen and Specialists, Opera Wonyosi*), London: Methuen,
  1984.
A Play of Giants, London: Methuen, 1984.
Requiem for a Futurologist, London: Rex Collings, 1985.
From Zia, with Love, and, A Scourge of Hyacinths, London: Methuen,
  1992.

Other criticism

There is a very extensive critical literature on Wole Soyinka. The
following will provide a good basic coverage:

Etherton, M., *The Development of African Drama*, London:
  Hutchinson, 1982.
Gibbs, J., ed., *Critical Perspectives on Wole Soyinka*, London:
  Heinemann, 1981.
  Wole Soyinka, Basingstoke: Macmillan, 1986.
Jeyifo, B., *The Truthful Lie: Essays in a Sociology of African Drama*,
  London: New Beacon Books, 1985.
Jones, E., *The Writing of Wole Soyinka*, London: Heinemann, 1981.
Katrak, K., *Wole Soyinka and Modern Tragedy*, Westport: Greenwood,
  1986.
Moore, G., *Wole Soyinka*, London: Evans Bros, 1971.

Ogunba, O., *The Movement of Transition: a Study of the Plays of Wole Soyinka*, Ibadan: Ibadan University Press, 1975.

Ricard, A., *Theatre and Nationalism: Wole Soyinka and LeRoi Jones*, Ile-Ite, Nigeria: University of Ife Press, 1983.

Whitaker, T., 'Wole Soyinka' in Bruce King, ed., *Post-Colonial English Drama.*

A useful source of information about and critical discussion of many aspects of Nigerian theatre is provided by:

Ogunbiyi, Y., *Drama and Theatre in Nigeria: a Critical Source Book*, Lagos, Nigeria: Nigeria Magazine, 1981.

For an excellent bibliography of African theatre see:

Gray, J., *Black Theatre and Performance: a Pan-African Bibliography*, Westport: Greenwood Press, 1990.

Athol Fugard and the South African 'workshop' play

Primary sources

With Kani J., and Ntshona, W., *Statements: Three Plays* (containing *Sizwe Bansi is Dead, The Island*, and *Statements After an Arrest Under the Immorality Act*), Oxford: Oxford University Press, 1974.

Dimetos and Two Early Plays (also contains *Nongogo* and *No-good Friday*), Oxford: Oxford University Press, 1977.

Boesman and Lena and Other Plays (which also contains *Blood Knot, People* Are *Living There*, and *Hello and Goodbye*), Cape Town: Oxford University Press, 1980.

A Lesson From Aloes, Oxford: Oxford University Press, 1981.

The Road To Mecca, London: Faber & Faber, 1985.

A Place With The Pigs, London: Faber & Faber, 1988.

My Children! My Africa!, London: Faber & Faber, 1990.

Playland, London: Faber & Faber, 1993.

See also:

Benson, M., ed., *Notebooks 1960/1977*, London: Faber & Faber, 1983.

Kavanagh, R., *South African People's Plays* (containing *uNosilimela, Shanti, Too Late,* and *Survival*), London: Heinemann, 1981.

Ndlovu, D., ed., *Woza Afrika!* (containing *Woza Albert!, Asinimali, Bopha,* and *Born in the RSA*), New York: George Braziller, 1986.

Other criticism

Coplan, D., *In Township Tonight!: South Africa's Black City Music and Theatre,* London: Longman, 1985.

Crow, B., 'Athol Fugard', in Bruce King, ed., *Post-Colonial English Drama.*

Fuchs, A., *Playing the Market: the Market Theatre, Johannesburg 1976–1986,* Chur and London: Harwood Academic Publishers, 1990.

'The New South African Theatre: Beyond Fugard', in Bruce King, ed., *Post-Colonial English Drama.*

Gray, S., ed., *Athol Fugard,* Johannesburg: McGraw-Hill, 1982.

ed., *File on Fugard,* London: Methuen, 1991.

Kavanagh, R., *Theatre and Cultural Struggle in South Africa,* London: Zed Books, 1985.

Orkin, M., *Drama and the South African State,* Manchester: Manchester University Press, 1991.

Sachs, A., 'When Art Takes Liberties', *The Independent,* London, 18 April 1990.

Walder, D., *Athol Fugard,* London: Macmillan, 1984.

'Resituating Fugard: South African Drama as Witness', *New Theatre Quarterly,* 3:32, November 1992.

Badal Sircar's Third Theatre of Calcutta

Primary sources

The following plays by Badal Sircar have been translated into English:

Marital: a Mini Play, in *Enact,* 44/45, New Delhi, 1970.

Shesh Nei (*There's No End*), in *Enact,* 59, New Delhi, 1971.

Baki Itihas (*That Other Story*), in *Enact,* 123–4, New Delhi, 1977.

Three Plays: Procession, Bhoma, Stale News, Calcutta: Seagull Books, 1985.

Evam Indrajit, reprinted in *Three Modern Indian Plays*, New Delhi: Oxford University Press, 1989.

Beyond the Land of Hattamala, reprinted in *Beyond the Land of Hattamala and Scandal in Fairyland*, Calcutta: Seagull Books, 1992.

See also:

The Third Theatre, Calcutta: Badal Sircar, 1978.

The Changing Language of Theatre, New Delhi: Indian Council for Cultural Relations, 1982.

'A Letter from Badal Sircar', *TDR*, 26:2, 1982.

'Our Street Theatre', *Sangeet Natak*, July–September 1983.

Other criticism

For more information on the development of theatre in Bengal see:

Raha, K., *Bengali Theatre*, New Delhi: National Book Trust, 1978.

For information on jatra try:

Gargi, B., *Folk Theatre of India*, Calcutta: Rupa & Co., 1991.

The best account of contemporary political theatre in Bengal is undoubtedly:

Bharucha, R., *Rehearsals of Revolution, The Political Theater of Bengal*, Calcutta: Seagull Books, 1983.

See also:

Van Erven, E., *The Playful Revolution*, Indianapolis: Indiana University Press, 1992.

Also:

Banfield, C., 'Badal Sircar' in T. Chevalier, ed., *Contemporary World Writers*, London: St James Press, 1993.

　'Stale News and Us, Two Intercultural Experiments', in O. Taxidou, and C. McCullough, eds., *Studies in Theatre Production*, Chippenham: Antony Rowe, December 1993.

Noble Dass, V., 'Experiment and Innovation in Modern Indian Drama in Translation: the Plays of Mohan Rakesh, Badal Sircar, Vijay

Tendulkar and Girish Karnad' in S. Pandey and F. Taraporewala, eds., *Contemporary Indian Drama*, New Delhi: Prestige, 1990.

Rea, K., 'Theatre in India: the Old and the New, Part Three', *Theatre Quarterly*, 8:32, pp. 47–66.

Richmond, F. P., Swann, D. L., and Zarilli, P. B., *Indian Theatre*, Honolulu: University of Hawaii Press, 1990.

Schechner, Richard, *Performative Circumstances from the Avant Garde to Ramlila*, Calcutta: Seagull Books, 1983.

Girish Karnad and an Indian theatre of roots

Primary sources

The following plays by Girish Karnad have been translated into English:

Tughlaq, Madras: Oxford University Press, 1972.*

Hayavadana, Calcutta: Oxford University Press, 1975.

Nāga-Mandala, New Delhi: Oxford University Press, 1990.

Talé-danda, New Delhi: Ravi Dayal Publisher, 1993.

A useful article written by the playwright is:

'Theatre in India', *Daedalus*, 118:4 (Fall 1989).

Interviews with the author, which have been useful in the preparation of this chapter are to be found in:

Anantha Murthy, U. R., *Enact*, New Delhi, June 1971.

Bandyopadhyay, S., ed., *Rangvarta*, 51, February 1991.**

Jain, M., *India Today*, 15 March 1992, pp. 68–69.

Other criticism

Awasthi, S., ' "Theatre of Roots", Encounter with Tradition', *TDR*, 33:4 (T124).

---

* *Tughlaq* is also published in *Three Modern Indian Plays*, New Delhi: Oxford University Press, 1989.

** *Rangvarta* is the news bulletin of the theatre research centre in Calcutta, the Natya Shodh Sansthan, based at 4 Lee Road, Calcutta, 700 020.

Raykar, S. S., 'The Development of Girish Karnad as a Dramatist: *Hayavadana*' in S. Pandey and F. Taraporewala, eds., *Contemporary Indian Drama*, New Delhi: Prestige, 1990.

For more information on *Yakshagana* try:

Gargi, B., *Folk Theater of India*, Calcutta: Rupa & Co., 1991.

Karanth, S., *Yakshagana*, Mysore, 1975.

Rea, K., 'Theatre in India: the Old and the New, Part Two', *Theatre Quarterly*, 8:31.

For more information on *Natyasastra* try:

Banham, M., ed., 'India' in *The Cambridge Guide to World Theatre*, Cambridge: Cambridge University Press, 1988.

Gupta, C. B., *The Indian Theatre*, New Delhi: Munshiram Manoharlal, 1991.

Rea, K., 'Theatre in India: the Old and the New, Part One', *Theatre Quarterly*, 8:30.

Shekhar, I., *Sanskrit Drama: its Origin and Decline*, 2nd edn, New Delhi: Munshiram Manoharlal Publishers, 1977.

Tarlekar, G. H., *Studies in The Natyasastra*, 2nd edn, New Delhi: Motilal Banarsidass Publishers, 1991.

Index

Index

Index